MASTERING
JUDO

Masao Takahashi and Family

Human Kinetics

Library of Congress Cataloging-in-Publication Data

Mastering judo / Masao Takahashi ... [et al.].
   p. cm.
 Includes index.
 ISBN 0-7360-5099-X (soft cover)
1. Judo. I. Takahashi, Masao, 1929-
GV1114.M375 2005
796.815'2--dc22

                      2004029108

ISBN: 0-7360-5099-X

The Web addresses cited in this text were current as of January 2005, unless otherwise noted.

Acquisitions Editor: Ed McNeely
Developmental Editor: Jennifer L. Walker
Assistant Editor: Mandy Maiden
Copyeditor: Amie Bell
Proofreader: Kathy Bennett
Indexer: Bobbi Swansen
Graphic Designer: Robert Reuther
Cover Designer: Keith Blomberg
Photographer (cover): Bob Willingham, International Judo Federation photographer
Photographers (interior): Barnaba Szluinski, unless otherwise noted. Photo on page viii © Kodokan Institute of Judo. Photo on page 3 © Roy Kawamoto. Photo on page 213 © Grace Hayami. Photos on pages 2, 7, 14, 18, 30-33, 36, 44, 68, 74, 78, 79, 81, 91, 108, 112, 114, 117, 118, 119, 125, 160, 163, 213, and 214 courtesy Takahashi family.
Art Manager and Illustrator: Kareema McLendon
Printer: Versa Press

Human Kinetics books are available at special discounts for bulk purchase. Special editions or book excerpts can also be created to specification. For details, contact the Special Sales Manager at Human Kinetics.

Printed in the United States of America   10 9 8 7 6 5 4 3 2 1

Human Kinetics
Web site: www.HumanKinetics.com

United States: Human Kinetics
P.O. Box 5076
Champaign, IL 61825-5076
800-747-4457
e-mail: humank@hkusa.com

Canada: Human Kinetics
475 Devonshire Road Unit 100
Windsor, ON N8Y 2L5
800-465-7301 (in Canada only)
e-mail: orders@hkcanada.com

Europe: Human Kinetics
107 Bradford Road
Stanningley
Leeds LS28 6AT, United Kingdom
+44 (0) 113 255 5665
e-mail: hk@hkeurope.com

Australia: Human Kinetics
57A Price Avenue
Lower Mitcham, South Australia 5062
08 8277 1555
e-mail: liaw@hkaustralia.com

New Zealand: Human Kinetics
Division of Sports Distributors NZ Ltd.
P.O. Box 300 226 Albany
North Shore City
Auckland
0064 9 448 1207
e-mail: blairc@hknewz.com

This book is dedicated to my father, Kukichi Takahashi
who provided us the opportunity to learn and study judo as a way of life.
And to my many teachers who devoted their lives to judo and its philosophies:
Atsumu Kamino, my first teacher,
Yoshio Katsuta, my sensei at the Buddhist temple in Raymond, Alberta,
Ichiro Abe, who guided me with his wisdom and superb technical expertise,
Katsuyoshi Takata, for his samurai spirit,
Keiko Fukuda, for her devotion to the purity of techniques taught through kata,
and many others too many to mention.
Finally, we would like to acknowledge our students, many of whom are now
sensei themselves. It is our hope that they continue to learn and to teach
and that they will surpass us in their ability just as our teachers hoped for us.

CONTENTS

Preface vi

Acknowledgments vii

Introduction: Kano's Art viii

CHAPTER 1   **Evolution From Art to Sport** 1

CHAPTER 2   **Traditional Values and Etiquette** 11

CHAPTER 3   **Focus and Attitude** 23

CHAPTER 4   **Training Methods** 35

CHAPTER 5   **Breakfalls, Posture, and Standing and Ground Positions** 67

CHAPTER 6   **Control Grips and Grip Breaks** 89

CHAPTER 7   **Standing Combinations and Counters** . . . 107

CHAPTER 8   **Physical Preparation and Weight Control** 135

CHAPTER 9   **Match Plans, Competitive Strategies, and Tactics** 157

CHAPTER 10 **Self-Defense Applications** 169

Appendix: A Listing of Nage-Waza and Katame-Waza 195

Index 208

About the Authors 213

PREFACE

Mastering Judo focuses on advanced technical instruction for training and performance. The book encompasses the complex dichotomy of judo as a sport and martial art. Although many books published on judo are directed toward the beginner judoka, *Mastering Judo* is written for the judoka who has already practiced judo and acquired an introductory level of knowledge (has obtained promotion in belt ranking from yellow to green or 5th to 3rd Kyu levels). This book is intended for the judoka who is interested in competing and who also wishes to further his or her knowledge of judo as both a sport and martial art.

Mastering Judo provides selected techniques that you can apply in competition. The technical focus is on how you can apply these techniques by utilizing various grips, movements, setups, and combinations. Information is given on training methods; the utilization of strategy and tactics; and other considerations, such as weight control and nutrition and the importance of studying kata. The practicality of judo is depicted with selected self-defense techniques that you can apply outside the sport.

Mastering Judo is different from other books you may have read on judo instruction techniques because it is based upon decades of experience from one of the most successful judo families, the six-member Takahashi family, who among them have a total of over 200 years of experience and 31 black-belt degrees as competitors and teachers. The benefits of the book are twofold: First, chapters on history, philosophy, and self-defense present a broad base of knowledge on judo as a martial art. Second, the book provides specific information on technical skills and training that will help you advance to a higher level. We are confident that *Mastering Judo* will help you improve your practice, performance, understanding, and enjoyment of judo as an art and a sport. Your continued progress is valued and expected in keeping with the spirit of judo.

ACKNOWLEDGMENTS

I want to express my appreciation to my family, all accomplished and dedicated judoka, for their continued support throughout the years. My son, Ray, deserves the most honorable mention, for patiently compiling all the information and undertaking the enormous task of writing the initial draft of this book.

Special thanks to Reginald Y. Hayami, for his diligent work on the family and decorative photos.

Sincere thanks to the expertise of our friend, photographer Barnaba Szluinski, who, assisted by George Hambleton, graciously took the technical photos.

Thank you to Ed McNeely for the inspiration and opportunity to produce this book, and to Jennifer Walker for her professional guidance.

Finally, to all the many teachers and outstanding students who have contributed to making the dojo well-known throughout the judo world.

INTRODUCTION: KANO'S ART

The evolution of fighting arts was first documented in Japan, with the first samurai battles recorded around the mid-800s. At this time in history, forms of combat were designed for the purpose of maiming and killing, both with weapons and without. Fighting arts used by the samurai were practiced and developed over various types of terrain and weather conditions. For example, in a prolonged fight in heavy armor, an advantage could be gained if one's opponent was made to advance uphill facing the sun. As the fight descended, possibly to swampy terrain below, the ability to grapple and hold the opponent to drown him on his back was important. This can be represented symbolically by techniques still used today.

Takenouchi jujitsu originated around 1532 and evolved from the techniques and fighting methods used by the samurai, which form the basis for many jujitsu styles and systems of attack. The art of jujitsu reached its height in the 16th century, and numerous styles emerged with masters and teachers eager to promote their versions. Many of these styles were good methods of combat and self-defense but offered little else. The role of the samurai began to decline within Japanese society during the Tokugawa period. The decline accelerated with the arrival of Admiral Perry in Tokyo in 1853, and the Tokugawa period and the samurai finally ended in 1868.

Professor Jigoro Kano is considered the creator of judo.

Professor Jigoro Kano, the creator of judo, noticed the inconsistency in the jujitsu masters' teachings and realized no guiding principle could be found among the vast array of jujitsu techniques. Jujitsu was unsafe to practice with its kicks, punches, stabs, slashes, and twists of the limbs, and the fighting form was abused by those having ill will toward society (for example, thieves, ruffians, and prison guards fighting for money). As a result, people thought negatively of jujitsu, and it gained a poor reputation.

Inspired by his thirst for knowledge and his background in jujitsu, Professor Kano believed a more complete version of martial arts could be devised. He realized the educational value of the practice and study of martial arts techniques. He also envisioned physical and mental training that would have its own philosophy and objectives. At 22 years of age, Jigoro Kano created judo, taking selected techniques from jujitsu, modifying others, and adding his own. A main feature of judo would be the ability to engage fully in dynamic fighting without the fear of injury through randori (free fighting), which was not possible in jujitsu with its many dangerous techniques.

Kano thus mainly developed judo from jujitsu, which had many styles and schools. The word "judo" can actually be traced to 1724 when Masayori Inoue established Jiki shin ryo judo, the first school of jujitsu to use the term judo. Professor Kano preserved techniques he learned from kito ryu jujitsu, which would come to be known in judo as koshiki no kata (classical forms), that were designed for combat while wearing armor. He used techniques he learned practicing Tenjinshinyo ryu jujitsu from founders Masatomo Iso and Hachinosuke Fukuda. Professor Kano chose the term "Kodokan judo" to differentiate it from jujitsu, which had developed a negative reputation, with the hope that judo would appeal to a higher class of society.

Initially, followers of jujitsu expressed fierce opposition to judo and threatened its progress and development. Professor Kano was relentless in promoting judo, however, and he was able to develop a loyal following that included good fighters, a few of whom were later dubbed as "the four guardians": Yoshiaki Yamashita, Sakujiro Yokoyama, Tsunejiro Tomita, and Shiro Saigo.

A clash between old-style jujitsu and judo came to a head at the 1886 Tokyo Metropolitan Police Jujitsu Meet, which would decide which martial art would be used for instruction. The significance of the event would either propel the practice of judo forward and give it credibility or propel it into oblivion. The 15-man duel ended with judo fighters winning 13 head-to-head matches against jujitsu fighters, with the remaining two fights ending as draws. The decisive win gave judo practice the impetus to spread and take a strong hold as the new martial art of the times.

Thus, within a few years of its creation the technical aspects of Kodokan judo were well established. By 1922, the Kodokan Bunkakai (Kodokan Cultural Society) formed two mottos that would guide judo practice: "seiryoku zenyo" (maximum efficiency with minimum effort) and "jita kyoei" (mutual welfare and benefit).

Professor Kano carefully chose the name "judo" from two Japanese words: "ju" and "do". "Ju" can be translated to mean "gentle, supple, flexible, pliable, or yielding." The word "ju" is also found in the word "jujitsu". "Jitsu" or "jutsu" can be translated to mean "art" or "technique" and represents manipulating the opponent's force against himself rather than confronting it with one's own force. The second word, "do", gives judo a unique advantage in concept over jujitsu. "Do" means "the way" or "the path," and this part of the word judo implies an accompanying philosophy.

It is difficult to understand the full meaning of judo through a simple translation of the word. For instance, the word "gentle" to the Westerner may lead to misunderstanding of the conceptual definition of "ju". Although gentle can refer to being soft or passive, Professor Kano was not opposed to strength in and of itself but rather to the unnecessary expenditure of strength. Why swing a wooden paddle to hit a fly when a quick flick of a flyswatter can better do the trick?

"It is not how strong you are but rather how little strength you can use."

The understanding of "do" is more difficult to grasp. Translated as "the way," the meaning of "do" is about more than just the perfection of judo skills and their application. In sport, such as football, the objective is to win the game by scoring more touchdowns than the opposing team. Players attempt their best to win the game. The best players are those who are able to perfect the skills of football and perform them within a competitive environment. Such perfection can be considered an art—the ability to perform a variety of complex skills and techniques. The purpose would be to obtain the result of a win or to better one's statistics such as yards per run. This is where the sport definition of judo falls short and is not a "way," just as jujitsu differentiates itself from judo by only having the objective of defeating one's opponent by its application of techniques and holds.

To understand and pursue the "way," consider both the judo athlete and the non-competitor. Both can train for perfection and compete to their fullest (that is, to win). Yet, a difference exists in what a win means to them. The noncompetitor still tries his hardest to win, although he may not really care if he does actually win. The desired result in both cases is ultimately to achieve personal satisfaction and learn from the process of striving to do one's best. The noncompetitor as well as the judo athlete can follow the way through understanding the many life lessons that can be learned from both winning and losing. It is refreshing to see a champion like Yasuhiro Yamashita (Olympic gold medalist, 1984) following the way through winning and doing his best to display the utmost respect and humbleness in his many victories. Similarly, upon Dutch athlete Anton Geesink's gold medal win at the 1964 Olympics over Akio Kaminaga (of Japan), a Dutch supporter rushed toward the mat to celebrate. Geesink waved the fan back to prevent an overt display of victory and to allow Kaminaga the dignity he deserved upon his defeat.

With a guiding philosophy and a firm establishment of kata (prearranged forms) and techniques later to be modified and known as the gokyo (1895), a range of people found judo appealing. Jujitsu gave way to judo, and Professor Kano took full advantage of this evolution, always taking the opportunity to promote his new art. Professor Kano was successful ultimately in planting the seeds of judo worldwide.

Evolution From Art to Sport

The first dojo of judo, or practice hall, called the Kodokan, was established in 1882 at Eishoji, a Buddhist temple in Tokyo. As membership grew, Professor Kano, the creator of Kodokan judo, moved the dojo nine times to larger quarters to accommodate the growth of judo. The word "Kodokan" is derived from the following: "Ko" means "lecture" or "practice." "Do" means "the way," and "kan" means "a hall."

The Kodokan was relocated to its final location in the Bunkyo-ku district in Tokyo in 1958 and is now a modern building distinguished by a statue of Professor Kano at its entrance. With more than 500 mats in the main dojo, which was rebuilt to commemorate its 100th anniversary and dedicated in 1984, the Kodokan has lodging, study and research areas, a library, and a museum. Students from all over the world can practice at the Kodokan, as it is open to all judoka. The Kodokan is an educational facility and important symbol for acknowledging what judo is and why it was created. An analogy to describe the relationship of the Kodokan to judo is the relationship of Mecca to the Muslim religion.

The International Judo Federation (IJF) recognizes judo as the fighting form created by Jigoro Kano. Unlike some martial arts where different federations and styles are accepted, Kodokan judo is the recognized form that allows for standardization worldwide. The Kodokan ensures judo is promoted as Professor Kano created it and upholds its traditions, customs, and etiquette. Kodokan judo teachers stress the preservation of techniques. Grading is regulated so that every yudansha (black-belt holder) who is approved is recognized through the standards of the Kodokan.

The Kodokan upholds the traditions of judo as it modernizes in time. Many people who practice judo are looking for more than just a sport experience. People are increasingly turning to judo for training in self-defense, physical education, and sport. But they are also yearning for the old-fashioned traditions and high standards of etiquette and respect set by the study of Kodokan judo. Figure 1.1 details the chronology of key events in the evolution of judo, which cannot be covered fully in this chapter.

The Kodokan Judo Institute is located in the Bunkyo-ku district in Tokyo.

FROM THE KODOKAN TO THE OLYMPICS

As mentioned in the introduction to the book, Professor Kano was tireless in his desire to see judo accepted in the martial arts community. As a scholar, Professor Kano was educated, bright, and visionary. He understood that establishing judo as an Olympic sport would provide the impetus for judo to flourish not only in Japan but also throughout the world.

The practice of judo as a sport enabled it to gain more public attention outside of Japan. Contests were being held as early as the 1920s when some European countries, such as England and Germany, held team competitions. Rules were established to highlight the spectacular throwing over groundwork so that judo would be appealing to the spectator. The ability for competitors to engage fully without holding back out of fear of injury made judo appealing to many people. Many other martial arts could not replicate dynamic fighting because of their dangerous techniques, and practitioners of these other forms could only resort to kata-style practice.

Professor Kano became the first Asian member of the International Olympic Committee (IOC) in 1909. The professor's persistence over decades paid off, and in 1938 the IOC decided that judo would be included in the 1940 Games scheduled for Tokyo. Around this time, judo was firmly entrenched in Japan and its practice was spreading quickly across the continents. Sadly, however, Professor Kano was unable to witness the fruits of his labor. He died of pneumonia at age 78 during his return voyage from the IOC meeting in Cairo, and the 1940 Games were cancelled because of World War II.

The proliferation of judo suffered a further setback in 1945 when its practice was prohibited by the postwar Allied occupation in Japan. U.S. General Douglas MacArthur believed judo and its followers threatened the Allied movement so he banned all judo and closed down all martial arts dojos (self-defense schools). MacArthur saw judo as being too militaristic, and he decreed that judo was not to be practiced and taught in schools. As far away as the United States and Canada many dojos were closed. As a result of societal paranoia, 110,000 persons of Japanese origin were relocated away from the U.S. west coast and 22,000 were evacuated outside the 100-mile protected zone along the west coast of Canada and many placed in internment camps. Judo was in jeopardy of losing much of what it had gained over the years in terms of development and progress.

In both Canada and the United States there was discrimination against people of Japanese decent, many of whom were born on North American soil. In the United States, judo instructors were rounded up

Judoka at POW Camp 101 located in Angler, Canada. Left to right: Nobuyoshi Kawano, Sadami Ozaki, Masato Ishibashi, and Eiichi Yoshikuni.

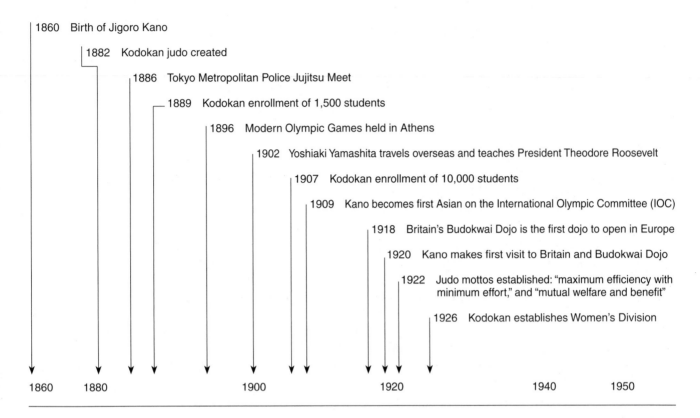

1860   Birth of Jigoro Kano

1882   Kodokan judo created

1886   Tokyo Metropolitan Police Jujitsu Meet

1889   Kodokan enrollment of 1,500 students

1896   Modern Olympic Games held in Athens

1902   Yoshiaki Yamashita travels overseas and teaches President Theodore Roosevelt

1907   Kodokan enrollment of 10,000 students

1909   Kano becomes first Asian on the International Olympic Committee (IOC)

1918   Britain's Budokwai Dojo is the first dojo to open in Europe

1920   Kano makes first visit to Britain and Budokwai Dojo

1922   Judo mottos established: "maximum efficiency with minimum effort," and "mutual welfare and benefit"

1926   Kodokan establishes Women's Division

1860   1880   1900   1920   1940   1950

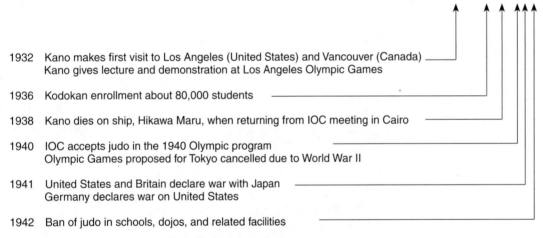

1932   Kano makes first visit to Los Angeles (United States) and Vancouver (Canada)
       Kano gives lecture and demonstration at Los Angeles Olympic Games

1936   Kodokan enrollment about 80,000 students

1938   Kano dies on ship, Hikawa Maru, when returning from IOC meeting in Cairo

1940   IOC accepts judo in the 1940 Olympic program
       Olympic Games proposed for Tokyo cancelled due to World War II

1941   United States and Britain declare war with Japan
       Germany declares war on United States

1942   Ban of judo in schools, dojos, and related facilities

Figure 1.1 Chronology of key events in judo.

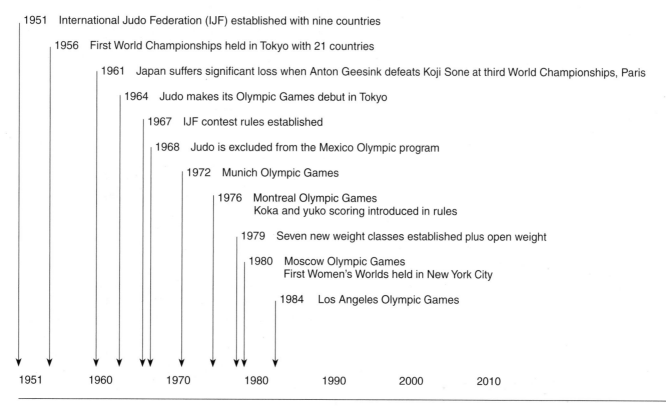

1951   International Judo Federation (IJF) established with nine countries

1956   First World Championships held in Tokyo with 21 countries

1961   Japan suffers significant loss when Anton Geesink defeats Koji Sone at third World Championships, Paris

1964   Judo makes its Olympic Games debut in Tokyo

1967   IJF contest rules established

1968   Judo is excluded from the Mexico Olympic program

1972   Munich Olympic Games

1976   Montreal Olympic Games
           Koka and yuko scoring introduced in rules

1979   Seven new weight classes established plus open weight

1980   Moscow Olympic Games
           First Women's Worlds held in New York City

1984   Los Angeles Olympic Games

1951   1960   1970   1980   1990   2000   2010

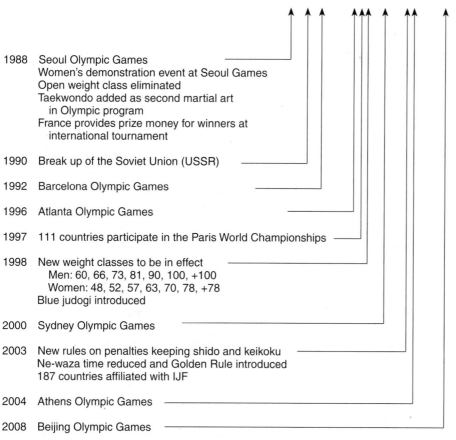

1988   Seoul Olympic Games
       Women's demonstration event at Seoul Games
       Open weight class eliminated
       Taekwondo added as second martial art
         in Olympic program
       France provides prize money for winners at
         international tournament

1990   Break up of the Soviet Union (USSR)

1992   Barcelona Olympic Games

1996   Atlanta Olympic Games

1997   111 countries participate in the Paris World Championships

1998   New weight classes to be in effect
       Men: 60, 66, 73, 81, 90, 100, +100
       Women: 48, 52, 57, 63, 70, 78, +78
       Blue judogi introduced

2000   Sydney Olympic Games

2003   New rules on penalties keeping shido and keikoku
       Ne-waza time reduced and Golden Rule introduced
       187 countries affiliated with IJF

2004   Athens Olympic Games

2008   Beijing Olympic Games

and sent to internment camps. Although judo was practiced within the confines of the internment camps, it virtually came to a halt in Canada and the United States. Interestingly, no internee was ever charged with a crime by the FBI or Royal Canadian Mounted Police (RCMP) during the internment period. And, ironically, many nissei (second-generation Japanese) fought for the United States while their families were confined in internment camps for no reason except racism. U.S. Senator Daniel Inouye won medals for bravery fighting for the United States during World War II in Italy. He was wounded many times, including losing an arm in battle.

Despite these setbacks, the practice of judo continued to evolve, albeit slowly, just as Professor Kano would have wished. In 1948 the first postwar All-Japan Judo Championships were held, and the following year the All-Japan Judo Federation was established. After the war, judo teachers focused on teaching judo as a sport with an educational basis, in part to deemphasize the martial art for self-defense aspect and to ultimately regain inclusion in the Olympic Games.

Judo was also taking hold in many countries in Europe, and in 1951 the International Judo Federation (IJF) was established. By this time, regular international competitions were being held in Europe and spreading elsewhere. The first World Judo Championships were held in Tokyo in 1956 with 21 countries in attendance.

A turning point to the acceptance of judo into the Olympic Games was the successful hosting of the 1958 Asian Games in Japan. The Japanese quickly focused their efforts to get judo into the 1964 Games. Their efforts were helped by the IJF, who asked each member country to appeal to its own Olympic Committee to lobby for the inclusion of judo in the 1964 program.

The teaching of judo as a sport was growing rapidly, and its inception in the 1964 Olympic Games in Tokyo was a significant event. The 1964 Games were the first to be televised and offered a chance for Japan to show judo to the world and to highlight Japanese dominance in the sport. After considerable debate on what weight classes to

Spirit Is Victorious

In the years leading up to the 1964 Olympics, Japanese traditionalists resisted weight classes, believing instead that regardless of weight the most skilled judoka would always emerge victorious. Masao Takahashi embodied the spirit of the open-weight category. He would often enter the open division, where judoka of any weight can enter. In a Detroit tournament in 1959, Takahashi took on the "big men," and his impressive showing was described by Frank Moritsugu in the *New Canadian* as a triumph of technique over size both in throwing and in avoiding being thrown or pinned by doing the Mifune trick of riding his opponent and avoiding be-ing thrown by floating around him (June 29, 1959).

Because of his size and strength, as well as his technique, Anton Geesink of Holland dispelled the myth that strength was immaterial by winning the 1961 World Championships in Paris by beating Koji Sone of Japan. Many believe Sone was the technically better judoka although Geesink was regarded highly as well. It would be the last time the World Championships would be an open-weight event. Implementing weight classes became a harsh reality for judo traditionalists, especially when it was realized that having them was the only hope of having judo enter the Olympic program.

use, four divisions were contested: light (under 68 kilograms [150 pounds]); middle (under 80 kilograms [175 pounds]); heavy (over 80 kilograms [175 pounds]); and the open weight class, where any competitor of any weight could enter. Japan took all weight divisions that year except the open division, which was won by Anton Geesink of Holland. The bigger and stronger Geesink beat Japan's Akio Kaminaga with a smothering kesa-gatame (hold-down).

Anton Geesink's victory for Holland at the 1964 Games prevented a sweep by Japan and was important for the further progress of judo. Geesink, who trained in Japan, was highly respected and did much to promote the sport. His win symbolized the ability of non-Japanese to excel in judo and provided inspiration for others to follow suit. The success of other nations in judo, despite the dissatisfaction of the Japanese, was good for the sport. A Japanese-dominated martial art created by the Japanese would have more difficulty being accepted by other nations if others believed that their success was improbable.

The fast growth of judo outside of Japan was in large part a result of judo being accepted as an Olympic event. Many sport federations sought to gain prestige and international recognition for their home countries as a result. Although judo was excluded from the 1968 Games in Mexico, the sport was again included in the Munich Games of 1972 and has been a part of every Olympics since.

Another key moment in the evolution of judo was the inclusion of women in the sport. The first World Championships for women were held in 1980 in New York City. Women's judo gained Olympic status in Seoul as a demonstration sport in 1988. Women competed in judo officially in the Barcelona Games of 1992. Ingrid Berghmans, Olympic champion from Belgium is considered among the best female competitors ever, while Tina Takahashi, Olympic coach for Canada in 1988, did much to further promote women's judo, particularly in Canada.

Some of the biggest changes to judo have occurred as a result of its inclusion in the Olympics. In fact, judo as an Olympic event now has to contend with conditions such as spectator appeal, and the IJF has been continually modifying judo rules as a result. The differentiation between judo as sport and judo as martial art became more prevalent as a result. (See figure 1.2.)

In 1984 Tina Takahashi became the first Canadian to win a judo gold medal at a World Championship event. She is pictured here at the 1984 World University Championships.

INTERNATIONALIZATION OF JUDO AS A SPORT

The internationalization of judo is likely one of the most phenomenal of any Olympic sport. Judo is truly practiced worldwide, and this spread has been a direct result of the rapid development of judo as a sport. The beauty of this spread has been the dissemination of a judo that is standardized in its teachings. The IJF clearly states that it recognizes judo as that of Kodokan judo. What this means is that if you visit a dojo in the United States, France, or China, you will find that the judo being taught is the same—Kodokan judo. Currently, more than 187 national judo federations are

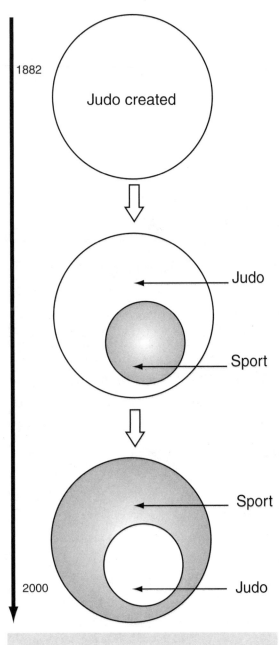

1882

Judo created

Judo

Sport

Sport

2000 · Judo

Figure 1.2 Evolution of judo as a sport.

affiliated with the IJF, the official organization for Olympic participation, making judo one of the largest representative sports. Professor Kano's vision of judo becoming an international sport can truly be acknowledged.

Although Japan is still considered the dominant country in judo because of its depth of high-caliber fighters, the spread of judo has enabled many countries to find success as measured through the Olympic Games and World Championships. The distribution of success throughout all parts of the world has helped the sport of judo thrive and continually develop worldwide. It is said that judo is one of the most practiced sports in the world with more than 20 million participants.

Judo parity can be viewed by how competitive the sport is from an international perspective. Despite the accepted dominance of judo by Japan, the medal count by other nations at the Olympic Games indicates parity among countries. Even in judo's inauguration at the Tokyo Olympics in 1964, nine countries collected Olympic judo medals—a good start, considering that there were only four weight divisions. In recent times, with the inclusion of women and the increased number of weight divisions, judo's global parity is even more apparent. In the 2004 Summer Olympics in Athens, for example, 26 different countries took home medals in judo.

The reasons for parity in judo are complex but can be narrowed to some key factors. When the Soviet Union broke up in the early 1990s, judo immediately became more competitive at the elite level because many of the Soviet republics have strong roots in combative sports. The sheer number of countries practicing judo (187 plus) indicates judo is practiced globally, so its competitiveness is gauged internationally by what's happening. Coaching and instruction also have improved along with training methods that further develop the talent pool. The attractiveness of judo for children helps in developing a strong young talent base so the transition to senior levels can be made easier. It is not uncommon for junior-level athletes to do well in senior competition even at the elite level.

REFOCUSING FOR THE FUTURE

The teaching of judo as a sport became an effective way to introduce it to the public. People could understand sport, and judo as a sport spread throughout the world quickly. As we have seen, from its inception and Professor Kano's dream to see judo as an event in the Olympic Games, judo has become increasingly important to many national sport federations. Emphasis on elite sport created systems of development for judo, including an increased number of international competitions, better training facilities and centers, higher-quality coaching support, and leagues. This continued support structure by nations vying for international and Olympic gold provides a forum in which athletes can be expected to train year round with a full-time commitment.

It is ironic that Professor Kano promoted judo as a sport so that it would gain acceptance internationally. But those who love judo must take note that a heavy sport focus can alter judokas' behavior so drastically that it can override all other aspects of judo's teachings. This attitude is contrary to the very fundamental philosophy of judo (described next) that Professor Kano believed distinguished it from other martial arts.

"Jita kyoei," or "mutual welfare and benefit," is one of two mottos (the other being "seiryoku zen'yo," or "maximum efficiency with minimum effort") that provide the basis of direction that ultimately will affect the behavior and actions of the judoka. One cannot be selfish if operating out of jita kyoei. The judoka must work together with his or her partner to accrue mutual benefit through judo. In randori training, for example, which looks like a fight, there is "giving" to one's uke (partner who receives the action) so that mutual benefit can be obtained. Even with full resistance, the dynamic actions of randori resemble an all-out match, yet the attitude of the true judoka is far from that of winning at all costs. The concept of jita kyoei is confusing and sometimes difficult for the beginner judoka and Western thinkers to grasp. Understanding this philosophy reveals much of what jita kyoei is all about.

The sport focus eliminates the need for jita kyoei. In sport, the athlete wants to win and the elite athlete can obtain that objective with a sport focus that narrows as it becomes more specialized. In many respects, to obtain elite status, one must be selfish because everything must be directed to the good of the individual aspiring athlete. The emphasis on competition narrows the teaching of judo, and the judo athlete is taught judo only as a sport. As a result, parts of judo are disregarded or de-emphasized. For example, instances of proper bowing are sometimes neglected in the tournament environment. Fighters bow with their feet apart and arms dangling from their sides, and they simulate a bow with a quick forward jerk of the body. The judo traditionalist would shudder at such a display of disrespect for the very act of showing respect for mutual welfare and prosperity. But, little blame can be placed on the fighter who is so focused on the fight and was likely never taught to bow properly and even perhaps will never be corrected.

Michel Brousse and David Matsumoto (*Judo. A Sport and Way of Life*. Ed. International Judo Federation. 1999. Korea. Pg. 113.) speak about the "sportification" of judo. They provide the following optimistic statement: "Today the judo world has matured and the abuses of the sport orientation are now compensated by an equal interest in the educational aspects of judo."

In many cases, the value of judo for the education of people is not overlooked. More and more in Western culture, there is a need for sporting activities that can provide more than the skills of the game. In fact, many of the qualities that sport judo can bring out in the individual are the same types of qualities that can be acquired through the motto "jita kyoei." Sportsmanship, a Western term, is a concept that mirrors the teachings of judo on how to act honorably as a result of involvement in sport. (For a further discussion of attitude, see chapter 3.) George Kerr, a highly respected fighter, coach, and authority on judo from Scotland and an 8th Dan, provides a cautionary perspective: "If such courtesy is not maintained and the needs of competition prevail, judo will suffer and decline, as has happened in other Western sports."

There is no question, however, that the development of judo was a result of the application of judo as a sport. Traditionalists and modernists struggled with its evolution, yet it was inevitable that change would occur. However, as Masao Takahashi, 8th Dan, remarks: "Running the dojo for only fighters is not good for judo. You have to teach judo as a martial art." Similarly, June Takahashi believes the teachings of the Kodokan tradition and history should be taught to all judoka. Further discussion of proper judo etiquette is covered in chapter 2.

The values of judo philosophy and tradition, such as jita kyoei and mutual welfare and benefit, are crucial. Judoka must learn to respect themselves, their bodies, their elders and coaches, higher-ranking judoka, and others. Students of judo should not only learn to be physically fit but also fit in spirit by concentration, dedication, and the ideals of mutual welfare and benefit. Masao Takahashi emphasizes the wholeness of judo: "We call judo a sport, but, really, it's the study of a culture." Read on to chapter 2 for more information on preserving the traditional values and etiquette of judo.

Traditional Values and Etiquette

From its inception, judo has upheld traditional values and high standards of etiquette. Professor Kano emphasized these aspects as an important part of judo, not only to differentiate it from other martial arts but also to fulfill the purpose of developing the overall judoka and person. Some rules are closely linked to etiquette and are implemented within competition.

On and off the mat, etiquette is likely the most important aspect of judo. Etiquette can be described as rules, customs, or ways to conduct oneself within judo. Much of judo etiquette involves unwritten rules. Many other sports, some more than others, implement etiquette. For example, in the sport of golf, etiquette is deemed important not only for the players but also for the spectators. When a player tees off it is customary that spectators stay quiet and still and that they refrain from taking photographs that can disrupt the player's concentration. In judo, the bow taken toward one's opponent before the match is a visible procedure of etiquette that represents mutual respect.

Two of the main purposes of etiquette are efficiency and safety. Efficiency refers to the judoka's conduct and the ability to operate in an effective manner. The formal start and finish of practice (bowing in and out), for example, are a form of etiquette that ensures that everyone is punctual, orderly, and prepared to start the practice session. The bow also is a show of respect to one's practice partners as an expression of thanks for participating in the practice or match so that each partner can improve skills. Safety etiquette in judo is important, and strict rules limit the risk of injury, especially in activities such as randori, or free-practice fighting.

Etiquette serves another important role in judo that distinguishes it from other combative activities and martial arts. The emphasis on etiquette maintains perspective with regard to the higher aims of judo, which was also created to educate and develop the overall person within society. This perspective is especially important today when so much emphasis is placed on winning. Maintaining etiquette in judo does not necessarily mean that the judoka downplays the importance of striving to win. True judo champions are those who excel as high-level athletes and who display the respectful behaviors of Kodokan judo. In some respects, etiquette takes judo to a higher level than just being a sport in which the objective can be simplified to winning the game. Emphasis should be placed on building one's character along with one's technical ability.

EXPECTATIONS FOR RESPECT AND RITUAL IN THE DOJO

Many dojos have their own rules and most, if not all, have been passed on with the standardization of Kodokan judo. "Dojo," or "place where judo is practiced," originally comes from the Buddhist terms "do" (means "way or path") and "jo" (means "place of enlightenment or worship"). This definition helps us to understand the connection of the dojo and the practice of etiquette in judo.

There are certain rules that are common to all good dojo that you will be expected to know and observe. Study these well.

1. Students must be punctual at all scheduled meetings.
2. Students must wear traditional keikogi properly with a belt indicating their earned rank at all practice sessions.

3. Students must keep their keikogi clean and in good repair.

4. Students must keep their bodies clean and fingernails and toenails trimmed.

5. Students must not wear jewelry or any sharp objects when exercising.

6. Students must not chew gum or have food of any kind in their mouths while in the dojo.

7. Students must obey the instructions and respect the discipline of their seniors and instructors.

8. Students must practice only those techniques that have been formally presented by their instructor.

9. Students of lower ranks must seek to exercise with higher-ranking partners.

10. Students must not engage in idle talk while in the dojo.

11. Students must remain quiet and attentive when not exercising.

12. Students should always be courteous and helpful to each other. The Budo code of sportsmanship requires that the less adept in rank or physical condition be protected.

13. Students should help to keep the dojo clean and in good repair.

14. Students must use the correct form of standing or kneeling bows, when entering or leaving the dojo and to each other at the beginning and end of each session.

15. Students must sit properly while on the mat.

16. Students must always be serious, sincerely entering into the spirit of the art, especially during randori and contests. The spirit of fair play, obedience to the referee's judgement, and giving as much importance to the attitude of the match or practice as to the results, are of the greatest importance.

17. Students must know the rules of the contest.

18. Students must not misuse the knowledge of the arts.

The following are examples of expectations of dojo etiquette:

• Good hygiene is expected out of courtesy to others practicing judo. Not only should you maintain good personal hygiene, but also you are expected to keep your judogi (cotton uniform) clean and in good condition. You must wear footwear when leaving the mat, and only clean, bare feet are permitted on the tatami or in the practice area. Keep your tatami clean, and wash or wipe the tatami after each session.

• Proper sitting in the dojo is important for safety reasons. The two accepted sitting positions are kneeling (seiza) and cross-legged (anza), a less formal sitting method. Always face toward the center of the mat or action and avoid facing your back toward shomen, or the side on which persons of higher social rank or seniority are seated. Never lie down on the mat or lean back on straight or outstretched arms or legs. You could suffer serious injury if someone is thrown and happens to land on your outstretched arms. Another reason you must remain seated properly is to uphold orderly conduct and better appearance in the dojo.

• Bowing is an expression of respect and gratitude. Judoka partners bow toward each other before and after they practice. The bow represents expressing appreciation to your uke because one needs a partner to practice with in order to improve. Be sure to bow upon stepping on the tatami and upon leaving, and together with the class before and after the practice session.

A Judoka and a Gentleman

Ray Takahashi was thoroughly impressed on meeting Sydney Olympic champion Kosei Inoue of Japan only a few months after Inoue's Olympic victory. Takahashi dropped in to Inoue's training practice unexpectedly and was concerned that he was disrupting the Olympic victor. Takahashi recalls: "Inoue was in the middle of nage-komi and when asked to come over to meet me, he stopped, bowed to his partners, and approached me on the side of the tatami. As he bowed to me, dripping with sweat, you could see the sincerity in his bow and his politeness when Noriaki Kiguchi, a teacher at Tokai, introduced me as a guest. I thought to myself that he had just won the Olympics and had the courtesy to show respect to me—a visitor who just wanted to meet him. It was a nice display of judo by a champion fighter."

Left to right: Kosei Inoue, Ray Takahashi, and wrestling coach from Japan, Noriaki Kiguchi. This photo was taken during practice at Tokai University a few months after Inoue won gold at the 2000 Sydney Olympics.

Many other forms of etiquette are expected that relate to overall conduct and manners as an individual. You are expected to listen attentively during instruction and to learn by watching others if sitting on the side. During randori, you must fight hard to get the most out of practice. You are expected to respect higher-ranking judoka and your elders. Extend this respect to your fellow judoka as well because in judo one must cooperate and demonstrate appreciation and give-and-take during judo practice.

ETIQUETTE IN MODERN-DAY SPORT

As rules evolved as the sport of judo evolved, an attempt was made to maintain etiquette within competitive judo. Respectful conduct is expected whether one follows etiquette or rules, and both intertwine with each other. Around the 1950s, as judo was taking hold throughout the world, a conscious decision was made to preserve the tradition of judo in the construction of rules. It was deemed important that, along with maintaining judo traditions (including techniques), three other goals be met. These goals include keeping judo safe, promoting attacking judo, and maintaining the fairness between contestants.

Today, with the increased development of judo and the elite athlete, rules have become complex, particularly if one compares today's rules to those espoused in the first duel matches of the 1800s. The first rules established by Professor Kano reflected the needs of society to modernize while forging a national identity with emerging Western influence during the Meiji period in Japan. In addition, as the competitor becomes more sophisticated in adapting to rules, the rules have been adjusted to promote the active and dynamic judo that spectators demand to see. The introduction of the blue judogi in 1998, for example, was a significant change to better promote judo, which was resisted by the traditionalists who preferred keeping the judogi white to keep with tradition. Many proponents of the blue judogi (including IOC member Anton Geesink) believed it would provide the change needed to better expose judo to the media and the public. Those against the change (largely in Japan) believed it would erode the tradition that judo holds in such high regard. Traditionalists saw the temptation to change the color of the judogi as unnecessary and were wary of knee-jerk reactions that could permanently alter the sport and art.

Likely the most prominent changes in judo have occurred as a result of judo being practiced as a sport. In the beginning, final matches were as long as 20 minutes as opposed to today, when final matches last only 5 minutes and are shorter for women and for those under 20 years of age. Competitors used to kneel when fixing their judogi, and before 1976 there were only waza-ari and ippon scores (no koka and yuko). The impetus for change has been initiated largely by judoka in Europe, who are constantly attempting to improve the sport and make it more appealing to spectators. Implementing the blue judogi is an example of how the Europeans succeeded over traditional Japanese judoka who opposed it.

Much of judo etiquette and traditions have been maintained, however, in modern-day competitive judo. This preservation ensures the link of today's sport to the origins of judo. Some of these traditions include the following:

• *Bowing.* Again, bowing is a demonstration of respect, particularly by the judoka to the sensei (teacher). Bowing is a must for all competitors and officials in competition, and a guide to bowing is stated within the IJF rules. Judoka are not only expected to follow bowing customs in the dojo but also to continue such respectful customs off the mat.

• *Randori.* The training method of randori has considerable value that is applicable off the mat. The dynamic nature of randori's free movement without direct resistance to force allows the judoka to choose and pursue physical actions with consequence. If technical conditions are right, the judoka may be successful in his or her attack. Conversely, if a poor attack is initiated the judoka can be countered and fail. The uneducated observer may misinterpret randori as a "fight" and see judo as a violent activity, especially when both partners are of similar ability and weight and they fight to the maximum. However, randori actually teaches consideration for others because, if done correctly, both partners should benefit. If one partner is higher skilled then he or she should adjust his or her level down to use less strength and focus on defensive skills, combination, or secondary techniques to equalize randori. There is little benefit to either if the physically and technically superior partner continually dominates the other, which also portrays a selfish approach to learning judo.

- *Belt ranking.* Judo is unique to most Western sports in that a ranking system is in place for each judoka that is designated by the color of his or her belt. A white belt signifies a beginner, and a black belt indicates high proficiency. Progression can be based upon contest performance and technical ability. A person's contributions to the dojo, judo organization, and to others are also taken into consideration for promotion to the next rank. Kyu grades are designated for ranking below black belt, and Dan grades are for black belts. Although different countries may have some variations in color, the progression typically goes as follows starting with white for beginners and progressing to black:
    - White (6th Kyu)
    - Yellow (5th Kyu)
    - Orange (4th Kyu)
    - Green (3rd Kyu)
    - Blue (2nd Kyu)
    - Brown (1st Kyu)
    - Black (1st Dan through 5th Dan)
    - Red and white, or black (6th Dan through 8th Dan)
    - Red or black (9th and 10th Dan)

When a judoka achieves a black belt, the person becomes a 1st Dan holder and can progress upward. When 6th Dan is achieved, a red and white belt or a black belt may be worn. Ninth and 10th Dan can wear all-red or all-black belts (men and women must wear a solid-colored belt during competition). Some women, however, prefer to wear a black belt with a white stripe to preserve tradition and to distinguish women's judo from men's, although women do not wear a white striped belt in international competition. Performance in competition can be used to accelerate progression, after which factors such as service, experience, and contribution are valued.

Ranking serves several purposes. First, it clearly shows others the level of rank by the color of the belt worn. Lower-ranked judoka are expected to show respect to senior-ranked judoka. This seniority system is part of the etiquette of judo that is valued in other martial arts as well. Ranking provides a method of evaluating those judoka who are not fighters and competitively inclined. Placing value on acquiring technical proficiency is one of the great features of judo as it preserves standardization and promotes further study and practice. Within the dojo, ranking can serve as a safety mechanism by indicating the level of ability of others, which can be important in practice. A yellow-belt holder, for example, would approach randori differently with a fellow light-colored belt holder than if she were matched with a black-belt partner.

- *Terminology.* Using the Japanese language for various terms, techniques, and rules standardizes judo terminology. With a consistent terminology, techniques and original meanings are preserved that otherwise could be altered and adapted over time, particularly given the international influence on judo. Judoka worldwide, therefore, are able to know exactly what is meant and expected when one is to perform, for example, uchikomi (repetitive throw entries) or a specific throw, such as osoto-gari.

- *Conduct during competition.* The judoka is expected to display good conduct as a competitor and as a person, both on and off the mat. Proper conduct includes

A Case of Mistaken Identity

When Soviet fighters became interested in judo when it became an Olympic sport, judo was taught not as a system with great educational benefits but rather as another sport in which to gain medals. Soviet judo instructors had little regard for the traditions of judo because it coincided well with their own combative self-defense system called "sambo" (also written as "sombo"). Sambo had techniques similar to those of judo, and sambo practitioners also wear a jacket and a belt. Unfortunately, it was reported that the Soviets manipulated the ranking system against the Japanese at one of the earliest international tournaments by wearing belts of various colors that did not reflect their true rank. Not surprisingly, they did quite well despite their lack of etiquette with regard to the belt-ranking system.

following etiquette rules such as wearing zori (footwear) when off the mat and bowing when leaving the mat and to one's opponent before and after a match. Acceptable conduct also includes respecting officials and other seniors, such as other coaches.

COMPETITIVE RULES

It is fitting that tradition is upheld in judo competition, and records indicate the "Red and White" judo matches have been held in Japan since 1884. The Kodokan still holds the annual tournament, and it is considered the longest-held sporting event in the world. Although the rules in judo are far different today, Professor Kano established rules and had the foresight to document them, and some are still preserved in traditional competition. Similar to the rules of today, the early rules were established with objectives to ensure safety and fairness, to encourage action, and to make judo appealing to spectators.

Most tournaments use weight to classify competitors in categories. In younger age groups (below 20 years), age and rank are classified. Men and women compete separately from each other, although most tournaments hold men's and women's championships together so they compete alongside each other. International matches at the senior level are five minutes in duration, whereas children's matches can be as short as two minutes. The number of matches in which a contestant may participate depends on his or her advancement by winning and the number of competitors fighting in the same weight class. Usually, a winner may have five or six matches over the course of a tournament day.

Matches are officiated by a team of three officials. The referee conducts the match while two judges sit at opposite corners to each other. A "majority of three" is used for assessing scores, and penalties are recorded on a visible scoreboard operated by the scorer and timer. All terminology used follows the Japanese language and includes hand gestures. The contest area is a square and measures at least 8 by 8 meters (about 26 by 26 feet) and is no larger than 10 by 10 meters (about 33 by 33 feet). A 1-meter (about 3 feet) danger zone (in red) forms the perimeter of the square and is part of the contest area. A safety zone of at least 3 meters (10 feet) surrounds the contest area and forms the out-of-bounds area. At the start of a match, contestants bow to each other from designated marks on the tatami. The marks are placed 4 meters (13 feet) apart, with the blue competitor on the referee's right side and the white competitor to the referee's left. After bowing, the contestants wait for the referee to start the match by announcing, "Hajime!" (start).

Scoring

Once ippon (a full point) is scored, the fight is over regardless of the score or who was winning up to that point. Similar to the knockout punch in boxing, ippon can occur anytime; in fact, some matches have lasted only a matter of seconds. The rules of competitive judo have evolved to preserve the action and spectacle that features ippon judo. Ippon determines the match and is achieved by throwing, holding, or making one's opponent submit through an armlock or choke. If ippon cannot be scored over the course of the five-minute match, the competitor with the highest scores of waza-ari (half-point), yuko, and koka determine the winner. Matches that end with no score or a tie continue into an overtime period where the first score wins.

Ippon judo highlights the fighting attitude that a judoka possesses when competing. Judoka seeking to score ippon are typically offensive and possess a dynamic fighting style that is a pleasure to watch. Ippon judo is said to be derived from feudal times when warriors needed the spirit to end a fight to ensure their survival. Similarly, a judoka scoring ippon finishes his or her opponent off decisively.

Judo matches can be action packed, aggressive, and full of intensity. Some matches, however, vary in their presentation and can take a more defensive or tactical approach while still maintaining the competitors' quest to win. To the uneducated spectator, judo can be difficult to follow because of the numerous situations in which competitors can engage during the pursuit of victory. Although close or low-scoring matches can be exciting, there is pressure from competition-rule-making committees to make it appealing to spectators regardless of whether they are knowledgeable of the sport. Spectator appeal, unfortunately, is an important evaluation factor for Olympic events, and judo has fared poorly in the past.

Competition rules are constantly being reviewed to make the sport more attractive to spectators. At the 1997 World Championships in Paris, the rules as applied by the officials indicated startling statistics. It was recorded that for every two technical scores, one penalty was recorded. This high number of penalties was largely a result of the interpretation of stalling and noncombativity.

Allyn Takahashi throwing his opponent with left hidari seoi nage for ippon.

How to Score Ippon (Full Point)

- Throw your opponent on his or her back with considerable force and speed.
- Hold (osae-komi) the other contestant for 25 seconds.

- Apply an armlock, choke, or hold-down to make the opponent indicate submission by tapping twice or more or by saying, "Maitta" ("I surrender.").
- Score two waza-aris, which combine to score ippon (waza-ari awasete ippon) and can be obtained by scoring a throw or hold-down.
- Your opponent is penalized with hansoku make (disqualification).

How to Score Waza-Ari (Meaning "Technique Exists; Almost Ippon")

- You throw your opponent with control, but your technique is partially lacking in one of the other three elements necessary for ippon: largely on the back, speed, or force.
- You hold your opponent for 20 seconds but less than 25 seconds.
- Your opponent is penalized with keikoku or three shido-level penalties (explained later).

How to Score Yuko (Meaning "Effective"; Almost Waza-Ari)

- You throw the other contestant with control, but your technique is partially lacking in the other three elements necessary for ippon: largely on the back, speed, or force.
- You hold (osae-komi) your opponent for at least 15 seconds but less than 20 seconds.
- When your opponent is penalized with two shidos, you are awarded a yuko.

How to Score Koka (Meaning "Effect, Advantage"; Almost Yuko)

- You throw your opponent onto one shoulder, the thighs, or the buttocks, but not the back, with speed and force.
- You hold (osae-komi) the opponent for at least 10 seconds but less than 15 seconds.
- Your opponent is penalized with a shido.

Japanese Judo in Jeopardy

After Japan's questionable performance at the 1988 Seoul Olympics there was much talk of the future of Japanese judo. Some believed it was in jeopardy and would eventually be surpassed by other countries. Others believed changes in fighting style and strategies were needed. Most were not happy with how judo was progressing to where foreign fighters aim to win by accumulating the scores of koka and yuko. After much discussion and reflection, it was decided that ippon judo would remain the objective of Japanese judo. As 9th Dan Toshiro Daigo explains: "As long as we show traditional skill and take ippon, Japanese judo will be okay. Once foreign players recognize the marvelous Japanese style of judo, they will adopt the same route we are taking."

Japan's domestic tournaments still keep traditional rules that do not score the lesser scores of koka and yuko. This type of scoring encourages the judoka to go for ippon. At the Athens Olympics, Japan reestablished itself as a dominant nation, placing first in judo overall. One of the stars of the Games was Tadahiro Nomura, who won his third Olympics with a display of spectacular ippon judo.

Judo rules reward the quality of the technical score (for example, throw), so if waza-ari (almost ippon) is scored it is regarded higher than any number of yuko or koka scores (lesser technical scores). Similarly, any number of kokas, the lowest technical score, is not enough to beat a yuko score. Before 1976, waza-ari and ippon were the only technical scores recorded. The lesser scores of yuko and koka were added to acknowledge and keep track of any advantages the competitors acquired throughout the match.

Penalties

One of the main features of judo, the ability to engage fully yet safely, is what helped elevate it above other martial arts such as jujitsu. Given the combative nature of judo (throwing someone on his or her back to the tatami, bending back the arm, and so on), strict rules must be in place to ensure the safety of participants. Infractions to the rules result in penalties.

In 2003, the IJF Refereeing Commission proposed to simplify the penalties to only two levels of severity: shido (slight infringements) and hansoku make (grave infringements). The penalties correspond directly to the "positive" scores of ippon, waza-ari, yuko, and koka. That is, when a competitor receives a shido, one's opponent (the nonoffending judoka) receives the corresponding score of koka. Similarly, a second shido would result in the awarding of yuko to the nonoffending judoka, and a third shido would convert to the opponent's scoring of waza-ari. The fourth and final shido would result in hansoku make, or disqualification.

Hansoku make (disqualification)	*Ippon*
Shido (slight infringement)	*Koka*

Here are some examples of penalty infractions:

- Shido: "Negative judo," false attack, stalling, overly defensive posture, squeezing the opponent's trunk with leg scissors, applying a choke across the opponent's chin, applying a technique outside the contest area, intentionally fleeing the mat

The Rules

The rules, once set, allow the athlete and coach to come up with ways to best work within the framework to obtain the goal of winning. In other words, when the koka score was introduced it would be a matter of time before techniques were designed to just score koka. Judoka will adapt to the rules and even manipulate them to achieve the goal of winning. Techniques have been modified, and new ones have emerged as a result. No longer can the term "kuzure," meaning variation, be used to encompass all the changes that have resulted to the techniques in modern judo. Toshihiko Koga, who is credited with perfecting the "wrong" shoulder technique, sode-tsurikomi-goshi, has a personal maxim to follow "a new wind," or to maintain the openness to seek challenges with new approaches.

- Hansoku make: Intentionally falling backward when the other contestant is clinging to one's back, wearing a hard object (such as a ring, bracelet, or braces), intentionally endangering or injuring the opponent's neck or spinal vertebrae, taking actions that may be against the spirit of judo, such as disregarding the referee's instructions

Other penalties occur as a result of a judoka's failure to comply with rules of etiquette. A judoka who is not wearing a proper uniform or who disregards the expectation of hygiene can be turned away from competition and his opponent would then win the contest by "fusen gachi" (win by default) or, if the contest has already started, by "kiken gachi" (win by withdrawal).

Scoring and Boundary Lines

Considerable action occurs near the edge of the mat. There are many reasons for this. If one contestant attacks but is unsure of succeeding, the action can be inconsequential if it goes out of bounds. Some judoka play the edge of the mat and use it to their advantage (see chapter 9).

The danger zone (red perimeter) is part of the contest area. Once either contestant steps outside the zone or contest area (stepping on line is "in"), it is considered out and any technique applied is not valid (see figure 2.1). When one contestant throws his or her opponent outside but stays in long enough for the effectiveness of the technique to be clearly apparent, the technique will be considered in.

When a throw is started with both contestants inside the contest area, but during the action the contestant being thrown moves outside the contest area, the action may be considered for point-scoring purposes as follows: when the throwing action continues uninterrupted and the contestant executing the throw stays within the contest area long enough for the effectiveness of the action to be clearly apparent.

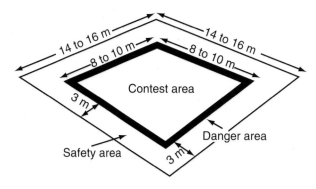

Figure 2.1 Observing the boundaries of the competition area is crucial in scoring.

If a throw such as ouchi-gari is attempted and the sweeping leg goes outside (grazes the safety area), the throw will be valid for scoring if the attacker did not place any weight on the foot or leg outside of the contest area. In ne-waza, the action is valid and may continue so long as either contestant has some part of the body touching the contest area.

Golden Score Contest

When the match is tied at the end; when the contestants have obtained no scores; or when kokas, yukos, and waza-aris are the same for each contestant, the match is decided by the Golden Score, where the first score or the first penalty awarded wins. The Golden Score is probably the most exciting recent rule change because it provides overtime sudden victory. This scoring eliminates the yusei gachi (win by decision) made by the officials and leaves the final win in the hands of the competitors.

COMMON TERMINOLOGY OF A JUDO MATCH

Hajime	*Start*
Matte	*Stop, break*
Sono mama	*Do not move, freeze action*
Yoshi	*Carry on, continue*
Osae-komi	*Hold-down is effective*
Toketa	*Hold-down is broken*
Sore made	*That is all, end of the match*
Hantei	*Request for decision*
Sogo gachi	*Compound win (for example, waza-ari plus keikoku)*
Jikan	*Time-out*
Maitta	*"I give up" or "I surrender"*

With etiquette and scoring firmly grasped, turn to chapter 3 to enhance your training with the proper focus and attitude.

Focus and Attitude

Professor Kano was explicit in identifying that mental training in judo is equal in importance to physical training. Kano intended that judo should be a system for both moral and educational development. These objectives are relevant to both the competitive and noncompetitive judoka. Serious study in judo requires a great deal of dedication, focus, and discipline that must be instilled and maintained to develop a sound psychological makeup.

Three types of attitude are discussed next: training attitude, competitive attitude, and personal attitude. First, training attitude refers to your willingness to train and the work ethic that you develop through regular practice. Second, a competitive attitude refers to your psychological makeup before, during, and after a competition. And third, your personal attitude is the overall attitude you develop, which is a reflection of you as a person both on and off the mat.

TRAINING ATTITUDE

The training attitude reflects the judo "process" that you go through as a judoka. Much can be learned and acquired through judo's training process, and the most important aspect developed is your work ethic. Good judo takes time to develop. The perfection of technique, the acquisition of timing, and the ability to react in a dynamic setting take years of practice. Regular training is necessary, and you must understand that improvement will sometimes come slowly; to improve you must be patient and consistent. Some judoka enter tournaments without being well prepared or without regular training. Those with natural ability can do well at first. Eventually, however, taking a nonchalant attitude toward training will catch up to them, and they will lose to the better prepared. The adage "hard work pays off" is simple but must be adhered to with good faith because success is a product of solid preparation. Without exception, a sensei, or coach, looks for a strong work ethic in a judoka as one of the most important qualities for judo success.

If you do not work hard, you cannot expect to be successful. Only you know the level of effort you put out. Hard work may not pay off immediately, but you will experience some form of success either soon or at a later time. Lack of effort will cost you in some way, and success may occur when you least expect it.

Many judoka expect results or immediate rewards after a brief stint of hard work. Unfortunately, progress can be slow to attain; sometimes you may feel as if you are enduring a plateau or slump. When a training plateau occurs, you must maintain a positive attitude and have the patience and persistence to work through and out of it. Often, too, you may feel as if you are not improving even though improvement is actually taking place. Improvement in judo can be compared to paint drying in the sun. Paint dries slowly, and in the sun it may even look as if it is still wet. Although the paint looks wet, it has progressed and is drier; so, too, do you improve slowly but surely, although sometimes almost imperceptibly. Next are several strategies for improving the training process.

Practice Regularly

For the best chances to improve, you should engage in regular training. Regularity of practice refers to practicing on a continual basis. To maximize training and learning, avoid long breaks and irregular attendance. For example, consider the following:

Case 1: 20 practices spread out evenly per week over 40 days

Case 2: 20 to 25 practices sporadically scheduled "whenever" over 40 to 50 days

In case 1, when practices are spread out consistently over time, you are able to make adaptations and improvements because it is possible to make your progression continual after each expected training session. When practices are sporadic and unpredictable, as in case 2, you follow a haphazard practice schedule where no structure can be put in place. With irregular practice you are subject to greater inconsistencies and even injury, even if the total number of practices is similar in number to the consistent practice schedule in case 1.

It would be a safe assumption to say that all great judo champions have had an outstanding work ethic. To win at the elite level, hard work and dedication are a must. Training attitude, however, does not only apply to elite fighters; the noncompetitive judoka may train with similar dedication but for different objectives. A nonfighter may focus instead on perfecting other aspects of judo, such as kata or technique. Both require good training attitudes despite having different goals.

The attainment of perfection by both competitive and noncompetitive judoka makes judo attractive to many who develop strong training attitudes. Perfection in judo follows a tangential line so that learning is continual and, some say, impossible to achieve. Judo is a lifelong endeavor, and a good training attitude is required.

Understand Judo

It is important to know more about judo from all aspects, not just practicing and competing (randori and shiai). Unfortunately, many judoka lack the basic knowledge of judo history and why tradition is so important. Strive to become better educated in judo, which in turn will give you a better appreciation of judo as an art and a sport. Knowing more about judo allows you to approach it in different ways, which can suit your needs as you become more proficient.

Set Goals

Goals are not just for fighters. Those who compete naturally set competitive goals, which serve to motivate and provide focus to their training. Nonfighters are equally apt to aspire to achieve their goals. Whether you are a competitor or a noncompetitor, the act of pursuing your goals will inspire and motivate you to follow through on what you hope to achieve in your judo.

Learning Is Ongoing

There was a period when there was no living 10th Dan in judo. Unlike some martial arts in which there are countless 10th Dan and masters and experts everywhere, in judo, practitioners acknowledge that no one can achieve total perfection because learning is ongoing. Those in the "waiting" believed they were not worthy to deserve the highest level of 10th Dan. In fact, only 14 judoka in the history of judo have had the privilege to acquire a Kodokan 10th Dan, 5 of which were awarded posthumously. Such humility reflects the dedication needed for completeness in judo. The training attitude represents the mental quality required for aspiring to perfection.

Goals should be task oriented and of two main types—short term and long term. Goals also need to be realistic (get black belt in one year?) and multileveled so that meeting short-term goals can build toward meeting long-term goals (get brown belt first!). Performance goals are important but are not always good indicators of progress. For example, if you win a tournament (a goal) then your goal has been achieved. However, what if you only beat opponents who were at a considerably lower level? What if you actually fought poorly? Conversely, what if you didn't win the tournament but fought well or were eliminated by drawing the unexpected champion or was subject to poor officiating?

An alternative would be to establish goals over which you do have control, that is, goals that are unaffected by external factors. For example, make your goal to attempt and score on a combination attack—ouchi-gari and tai-otoshi. Or, your goal could be to control the match by cornering your opponent to fight in the danger zone.

Keep an Open Mind

Be receptive to learning from other sources. Teammates and senior instructors are the most practical sources of additional information and knowledge. Many good books, Web sites, and videos are now available. A word of caution is necessary, however; you must be sensitive to other teaching methods and even techniques, especially if they contradict what you were taught within the dojo. You can still listen and take information in, but understand that your loyalty remains with your dojo and sensei.

Balance Your Lifestyle

Judo is a way of life, but it should not *be* your life. It is important to maintain perspective and strive for balance with judo and other important aspects of your daily life. If you are a student, for example, then your studies should go hand in hand with your training because athletic and academic pursuits are a balanced approach to healthy living. Do not be afraid to engage in other athletic pursuits as well.

Balance also refers to proper prioritizing. This means ranking what's important and ensuring top-priority items get the attention they deserve. When peaking for a major competition you may focus more on competing and its preparation. During a slower off-season period, academic pursuits may take priority. Regular training, however, is always important. Sporadic training or long periods of inactivity in any endeavor is not recommended.

Make Sacrifices

You must be willing to make sacrifices, especially if you wish to pursue competition. You must choose to eat healthy, get adequate rest, and passs on a social event the day before a tournament.

COMPETITIVE ATTITUDE

The psychology of the competitive judoka can be complex and sophisticated. In fact, many elite competitors use sport psychology as part of their training program and receive counsel from specialists in the field. At the highest competitive level, major competitive events such as the World Championships or the Olympic Games, levels of stress and pressure will no doubt be high. But, in relative terms, even the inexperienced competitor can experience similar psychological conditions of stress in a local tournament. In that respect, all judoka, whether they are experienced fighters or beginners, should attempt to learn continually from their competitive experience. Fostering a competitive attitude is important to all who engage or wish to engage in competition. Next are some tips to keep your competitive attitude at its sharpest.

Believe in Yourself

You must believe that you will win. How can you expect to win if you do not believe that you can? Believing in yourself gives you a fighting spirit. Many great fighters speak of this quality. All champions achieved their success with the belief that they could win. This does not mean that they knew that victory would be easy. And certainly, if you are not "favored" to win, it can be difficult to believe that you can. But, in order to win, you must fight to win. As world champion Noboyuki Sato puts it: "Fight like there's no tomorrow."

Having a positive attitude does not mean that you have to view everything in a positive light. In fact, it may be wise to prepare by looking for things that could go wrong. By being prepared for challenges, you will not be surprised if difficulties arise, and you will be better able to deal with them in a more prepared way. Don't get caught, however, in a negative mind-set that is self-fulfilling.

Doubt to Defeat

Ray Takahashi recalls vividly how a negative mind-set led to defeat. At the wrestling event at the 1976 Olympics, his teammate, a world medalist, said that the only person he didn't want to draw first round at the Olympics was Yuji Takada, the Japanese defending world champion. Fate would have it that he drew Takada first and lost the fight. In preparing himself for failure, this world medalist had talked himself into defeat.

Prepare for Competitive Stress

There are different names or words that can be used to describe competitive stress. Nervousness, apprehension, pressure, uneasiness—but, whatever it's called, all judoka experience it to some degree, especially on tournament day before a match. Many say that the difference between the top four place finishers is "all mental" because all possess the technique necessary to win on a given day.

Even Yasuhiro Yamashita, considered the heavy favorite at the 1984 Olympic Games, was under a huge amount of personal pressure to win. How can that be? He was undefeated for seven years leading up to the Games. Yamashita cites in his 1993 book, *The Fighting Spirit of Judo*: "At the Olympics I was under heavier pressure than in any other previous competition. Two images of myself came across my mind when I was alone: One had me waving to a large crowd of spectators with a gold medal, and the other had me hiding in the changing room after being defeated."

Stress is normal, and a main reason for stress is because tournaments are very different from training. Even hard randori and matches within the dojo do not elicit the same stress that tournaments do. Much of it has to do with all the different aspects that are involved in the fighting experience, including traveling, making weight, staying overnight in a hotel, eating differently, seeing your opponent, being at a strange new competition site, and fighting in front of spectators. Tournament fighting is filled with distractions to which you are unaccustomed.

A certain level of stress is needed, however, before stepping out on the mat. You should be alert and on edge as well as highly focused because a fight requires that you make tactical decisions as well as engage in intense activity. Some sports, however, like shooting, require a relaxed psychological state. Here the athlete wants to slow her heart rate down so maximal focus can be acquired upon pulling the trigger. Conversely, the Olympic weightlifter must psych himself up to ready the muscles for a maximal lift. The level of optimal stress varies among individuals, so you will need to discover by trial and error the level of stress that works best for you. Most judoka have little difficulty getting emotionally "up" for their matches; controlling the level of stress so that it is at the most effective level, however, may be the key to using stress to your advantage.

You will get stressed because you are preoccupied with your performance and the result of winning or losing. Caring greatly about how you will perform often leads to feeling pressured. Some of the reasons you may feel stressed in a competition include the following:

- *Self-doubt.* You begin to lose self-confidence. Often, this loss of confidence involves comparing your abilities to those of your opponent. Negative thoughts such as, *I don't think my throws are as good as his,* create doubt, which increases stress. You can still experience high levels of stress even if you are favored to win but start thinking that you might not.

- *Fitness level.* You question your level of conditioning, thinking that you will be unable to fight hard for the entire length of the match.

- *Overall health.* You don't feel 100 percent well. Judoka are notorious for detecting (or imagining) things that are not quite right—"I didn't get a good sleep," "My back is a little stiff," "I feel a little sluggish, maybe I cut too much weight."

- *Control.* You think about things that are out of your control, worrying about the myriad of things that can play a factor in the match.

- *Outcome.* You think only of the match result, that is, winning or losing.

Rather than focusing on these "what ifs," direct your energies toward things that you can control. Try using key words or cues to help you stay focused, such as "be alert," "get your grip," "keep moving," "be calm," and "stay loose." If you are able to shift your focus away from the result to performing the task immediately at hand, stress may even help. Being stressed will not necessarily affect your performance negatively as long as you can direct your focus to determining what you have to *do* to perform.

The best judoka are able to channel their emotions and focus their thoughts on what they have to do in a match. Some judoka prefer to stay relaxed whereas others need more motivation. For example, an easy method for achieving either relaxation or greater motivation is listening to music that helps you stay focused and achieve a positive frame of mind. It is also worthwhile to learn about mental rehearsal. Many of the best athletes are not only more experienced, but also they are better able to stay in control by focusing on learned routines. Common methods used are positive imagery (for example, forming an image or picture in your mind of performing a specific technique well), positive thinking, and preplanned routines. For example, experienced judoka know exactly how to warm themselves up and find that following a warm-up routine helps them to focus. Try out different methods and determine what method of dealing with competitive stress works best for you.

PERSONAL ATTITUDE

Personal attitude reflects one's personal character. Your personal attitude is made evident through your behavior and actions, how you conduct yourself in practice, and how you conduct yourself off the mat in daily living. Personal attitude is closely related to the judo motto of jita kyoei—mutual welfare and benefit. Following judo etiquette is an important way to develop a good personal attitude.

Regular training and punctuality develop discipline and commitment. The give-and-take between you and your partner formulates cooperation, even when engaged in hard randori training. Few other sports or activities can boast of the unique relationships that develop between judoka, in spite of the combative nature of the activity. This is an example of jita kyoei.

Achieving a good personal attitude is one of the main purposes of studying judo. Professor Kano believed that judo is a form of physical education that exercises the body and the mind. He encouraged practitioners to "make best use of your energy and go forward together with your opponent."

Isao Inokuma, one of the greatest Japanese judoka of all time, shifted his focus after his competitive days toward kata (formal exercises). Inokuma believed training attitude can be transferred to daily life and should be applied with the same discipline. After he retired, Inokuma applied the spirit of judo to his daily living, saying: "I am putting all my enthusiasm and fighting spirit into my current work and keeping up my studies. Judo is not a sport to be engaged in only at the dojo." (*Best Judo*. Inokuma and Sato).

Practice Confidence, Not Arrogance

As noted in chapter 2, the etiquette of judo is compatible with the Western ideal of sportsmanship; poor sportsmanship is not often displayed by judoka. The importance of winning, however, and the meaning it has for the elite judoka is powerful. As noted earlier, you must be confident and believe that you can win. The way you project confidence, however, may range from confidence that is honorable to egotistical cockiness or arrogance. Egotistical cockiness can be described as being "in your face," stating: "I am the best," and taking actions that project that image. Highly competitive athletes must believe they are the best, so there's a fine line between confidence and cockiness. Those who seem arrogant are sometimes those who need to think that others believe they are great fighters. Although such displays of brash self-confidence reflect poorly on the sport, it is hoped that continued involvement in judo will eventually help such individuals find greater humility and respect.

Remain Composed

You must be able to control your behavior and direct your energy to the appropriate area. When competing, you are representing your dojo, team, or even province or state and country. Equally important, you represent yourself and the sport of judo.

It is therefore important for you to portray a positive image both on and off the mat. Your actions as a senior judoka are observed by others and have a particular effect on younger judoka, many of whom will emulate their role models.

Respect Wins and Losses

Positive winning is how one handles victory in an honorable and respectful way. This is closely related to sportsmanship, but the difference lies in not letting victory "go to your head." Some judoka fall victim to this attitude, and their personalities change after winning a major competition. They sometimes feel superior to everyone else. Positive winning is difficult to learn because it is rarely taught. An example of positive winning is when Isao Okano used katsu (resuscitation technique) to revive Lionel Grossain (France), whom he choked unconscious at the 1964 Olympics using okuri eri jime. Okano's actions of concern for Grossain's welfare took precedence over his immediate urge to celebrate his Olympic victory. It should be noted that the teaching of positive losing is much more prevalent. In a tournament, you could say that there is only one winner and the rest are all losers. Positive losing does not only mean to display good sportsmanship after losing, but also it involves the process of learning from your mistakes.

As you gain more experience and understand more about judo, you will realize a greater appreciation of what judo can offer—especially once you are retired from competing. Some say judo is a "way of life." Those who have understood the depth of judo have also allowed judo to provide direction in the development of their personal attitude. Tina Takahashi describes how judo kept her "on the right track" in her teenage years: "Judo gave me something to strive for and demanded discipline. Although it wasn't easy, looking back at the experiences I had, the people I met, and the places I went educated me more than any type of formal education. [Judo] has shaped who I am and what I do."

Tina Takahashi was Canada's first world champion in judo (World University Championships, 1984), the first Canadian woman to achieve 6th Dan, and the first Canadian woman to coach judo at the Olympic Games (in 1988).

APPLICATIONS OF JUDO IN DAILY LIVING

The application of judo beyond training and the tatami is far reaching. Parents involve their children in judo because it does not entail the roughness that other sports do, such as wrestling, and many find the focus on discipline and etiquette appealing. Judo study helps children boost their self-confidence and self-esteem and helps them to learn to control aggression by providing structure, discipline, and physical activity in a controlled competitive environment.

Two-year-old Adam Takahashi Macfadyen at a judo demonstration with his mother, Tina. Judo is an ideal activity for parent and child.

Judo has been shown to benefit other individuals and groups within society. For example, judo is especially well suited as a therapeutic activity for individuals with special needs. One study reported that judo's dynamic nature of contact with control is particularly helpful for children who are psychotic and have problems with interpersonal space. After taking judo, these children began to better tolerate physical contact and appreciate the consequences of their actions. Judo study by people with visual impairments has been reported as a favorable activity because the gripping and contact allow for control, which they otherwise lack in most sports and activities. The timing and "feel" that are so important in judo movement allow such individuals to fully experience judo's dynamic activity.

Many practitioners of judo use its concepts and philosophies to develop their own personal approach to best contribute within society. Nathalie Gosselin, 5th Dan, echoes the positive benefits of judo practice through a program called ECLIPSE (Education, Cooperation, Learning, and Inspiration, a Personal Self-Change Experience). She found judo significantly improved behavior among youth who had been involved in delinquent behavior. Gosselin, a Canadian Olympian in 1996 and coordinator of ECLIPSE, reported that judo helps create positive behaviors that are transferred off the mat into daily life. The structure and discipline of judo practice is used as a physical therapy program for youth who are at risk and who need to learn to manage their anger and aggression.

It is not only those in need, however, who can benefit from judo. Business leaders use judo to guide their strategies and way of thinking. In fact, the term "judo economics" was coined in the early 1980s as a strategy for smaller companies to battle bigger companies in order to defend from a takeover and to survive in the business world. Judo economics includes using tactics such as leverage, rapid movement, and flexibility—elements used on the mat by the judoka. James Kendrick, PhD, 6th Dan, and former Canadian National team member, combines his expertise

Former Canadian prime minister Pierre Elliot Trudeau, 2nd Dan, engages in randori with Allyn Takahashi during a Canada Day celebration, July 1, 1983. Trudeau helped to popularize judo in Canada.

in judo and business administration to teach top North American executives to raise the bar to tackle tough leadership issues in an extremely competitive and volatile business environment.

Judo instills a way of thinking that guides your actions on and off the mat. It could be said that some political leaders who have practiced judo have gained from its perspective, including Vladimir Putin, president of Russia, and former prime minister of Canada, Pierre Elliot Trudeau. Prime Minister Trudeau practiced judo at the Takahashi School of Martial Arts in Ottawa, as did his three sons. Prime Minister Brian Mulroney enrolled his children as well.

Judo as a form of physical activity and exercise lends itself well to daily living. Honorable behavior, appreciation for others, and the etiquette of judo transfer well off the mat. For example, the meditation of "mokuso" before the start and the end of class, although short in duration, helps reduce the stress of the day and clear the mind. Cooperation is always tested to the fullest with your uke where "give-and-take" must occur, and then conversely in randori, where contestlike conditions are necessary.

JUDO FOR WOMEN

Judo can offer many benefits both mentally and physically for girls and women of all ages and stages in life. The practice of judo develops almost all of the muscles in the body, giving the practitioner strength, power, flexibility, agility, and cardiovascular improvement. Girls and women learn how to move their bodies in both standing and lying positions in order to attack or defend attacks. They learn to overcome fears of physically aggressive attacks such as chokes thanks to the practices in judo. Because judo is practiced with a fully resisting opponent, a realistic experience is gained. Mental and physical training empower girls and women with more confidence, assertiveness, and concentration. Achievement in rank or belts and winning a competition further builds one's self-esteem and can often develop short- and long-term goal-setting skills.

Many women compete in the sport of judo. There can be great rewards as well as sacrifices that help build character from these experiences. Judo can push one to the limit both physically and mentally and sometimes emotionally, particularly in competitions when adrenaline levels are high. A fighting spirit and mental toughness can evolve by learning to withstand pain and to fight back. This is an especially unique concept for girls and women, as they often do not get this kind of exposure in their daily lives.

Female participation in judo is now very popular in Asia and Europe and is gaining rapid popularity in the rest of the world. With the inclusion of women in the Olympic judo program in 1988 many positive changes for women's judo have occurred at the domestic level in many countries as well as internationally, such as increased refereeing, funding, and competitive opportunities. The development of women's judo has been relatively rapid compared to many other sports, especially combative sports. The older sport of wrestling, for example, only gained women's entrance into the Olympic Games in 2004 in Athens.

June Takahashi, 5th Dan, has been heavily influenced by Keiko Fukuda, 9th Dan, the highest rank achieved thus far by a woman. Fukuda is the granddaughter of Hachinosuke Fukuda, the jujitsu teacher of Jigoro Kano. Takahashi believes many judoka do not see the totality of judo because of the emphasis on competition. She says: "Judo teaches us to be better

Keiko Fukuda instructs kata (ju no kata) with June Takahashi during her visit to the Takahashi Martial Arts School.

people—that's the main objective—not winning." Takahashi was one of the first Canadian women to be promoted to black belt and is still active teaching kata and techniques at the family-operated dojo.

In the early 1900's, judo was once regarded as a practice appropriate only for women in the upper class. These women took part in randori, kata, the learning of techniques and etiquette, as well as the study of judo theory. The extensive training women received provided judoka such as Keiko Fukuda a complete perspective on judo, more so than many men who focused their energies on competition. Fukuda's motto reflects her philosophy of judo: "Be gentle, kind, and beautiful, yet firm and strong, both mentally and physically."

Career women, moms, seniors, and young girls all undertake judo for varied reasons. Whether learning to fall properly and safely, getting a great workout, stress relief, learning katas, honing a realistic self-defense technique, or perfecting the many ground and standing techniques, judo offers women of all ages countless benefits and satisfactions. Judo can be done recreationally, for fun, competitively, for fitness, and for self-defense. Judo teaches humility, respect, courage, and so many other virtues. The spirit of judo, the etiquette, the camaraderie, and the philosophies make this an attractive form of activity for all women.

Training Methods

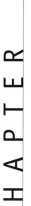

One of the most difficult parts of any athletic activity is determining effective training methods so that one can ultimately perform the skills and techniques successfully in competition. Competition is actually the best form of training because the judoka is doing exactly what is needed. To use competition only as a method of training, however, is impractical; in competition it is difficult to regulate and control factors such as intensity, volume of work, and level of competition. Too much competition can lead to risk of injury, unneeded stress, and incomplete technical training. Likewise, too much randori, or free fighting, can produce the same problems of training because randori closely mimics the dynamism of competition.

Training methods in judo have become more complex and sophisticated as the sport has evolved. There was a time when unorthodox and even excessive training methods in sport were more prevalent. Examples of excessive training methods include the judoka performing 1,000 push-ups a practice, the karate competitor breaking blocks of ice, and the wrestler carrying his partner while climbing up stairs. Even so-called sport-specific drills, such as thousands of uchikomi, form the mainstay of good, old-fashioned judo training. Despite the truth in the need for an exceptional work ethic, proper training is essential for any elite athlete, whether a judoka or otherwise.

Much of the success of Japanese judoka is still rooted in two necessary ingredients—hard training and depth of technique. Even so, effective training methods are essential for developing the judoka if one aspires to reach one's performance potential.

Secret to Success

Doug Rogers of Canada, who surprised many with his silver medal at the Olympic Games in 1964, was the first Westerner to be trained by the famous fighter, Masahiko Kimura.

After spending five years training in Japan, Rogers realized that the Japanese had no secret weapon but that their success was rooted in hard training.

Left to right: Masao Takahashi, Katsuyoshi Takata, and Doug Rogers at a special Kodokan training session.

And Japanese judo is still admired for its waza, or technical quality, which forms the benchmark of judo today.

This chapter focuses on specific judo training methods. Other training methods such as off-mat conditioning, although briefly discussed here, are covered in greater detail in chapter 8. The training methods presented in this chapter follow an important training principle—the specificity of training.

The specificity principle means that specific training produces a specific acquisition of results. That is, the judoka who does seoi-nage (for example, through uchikomi) will perfect those actions. A similar but different action, such as swinging an axe (which simulates throwing over the shoulder) will not train the muscles to act as efficiently as seoi-nage, but will train the muscles well for swinging an axe. If, therefore, you want to be good at judo or specific techniques, then you have to replicate the same type of training in practice. For example, in wrestling, it is common to see some facilities that use throwing dummies for the practicing of throws (koshi-guruma). Although this allows the full application for throwing (nage-komi), using throwing dummies does not replicate the specific actions because a throwing dummy does not feel and react the same way a person does (it is not realistic). Interestingly, throwing dummies are virtually never used in judo and are almost nonexistent in judo training, which specializes in throwing. Can those in the sport of wrestling learn anything from this?

Technical judo can only be acquired through judo-specific activities, such as randori and its related training methods. You should devote considerable time to these training methods and understand how they contribute to one's overall judo development. Off-mat training should be regarded as supplemental training and should not be used to replace your on-mat training methods.

A word of caution about off-mat training methods: In a weight-class sport, such as judo, and over an intense five-minute match, you can gain a significant advantage if you are more physically fit than your opponent. Off-mat training methods to improve one's physical fitness, such as running, do have their place in judo (see chapter 8). For example, weight training will improve strength, a needed component in judo because many actions engage large muscle groups against a resisting opponent. And, without a doubt, every elite judo competitor does some form of weight training. It has long been debated to what degree strength training should be part of a judoka's training, particularly if it allows less time for other training methods such as randori, uchikomi, and nage-komi. As mentioned in chapter 1, some judo purists believe strength hinders proper judo development and point to specific judo systems that emphasize a strength style of fighting, such as in Eastern European countries, where Neil Adams, one of Great Britain's best in the 1980s, remarks: "Perhaps nowadays there is a little too much emphasis placed upon physical preparation and conditioning, and with everyone rushing to get physically stronger, not enough energy is devoted to developing rhythm, balance, timing, proper positioning, and the use of your opponent's reactions" (*Modern Judo. Techniques of East and West.* Peter Seisenbacher and George Kerr. 1991. The Crowood Press. Wiltshire). The challenge for you is to obtain a healthy balance between proper technical developments and sound physical training to produce "good judo." It is well accepted that maximum development is best acquired when technical development has been achieved first. Be sure therefore to place an emphasis in your training on technical development.

The following example contrasts two methods of randori development. In case 1, technical aspects are developed first and then subsequently supplemented by extensive physical training. Once the technical aspects of judo have been developed, they are enhanced by the physical components, for example, strength and speed, and the judoka will reach his or her full potential. Emphasizing first your technique and then your physical fitness will allow you to acquire many of the fine-motor skills involved in techniques along with the timing and reactions that take years of practice.

| Case 1: | Technical | $\rightarrow$ | Physical | $=$ | Potential |
| Case 2: | Physical | $\rightarrow$ | Technical | $<$ | Potential |

It is true, however, that you can obtain faster performance success by first improving your physical attributes. This initial success occurs because significant physiological improvements can be made within six weeks (for example, improved strength), and physical training is "easier" than technical training in that little actual skill or talent is required. Case 2 indicates, however, that without a sound technical base one's full potential cannot be reached.

Wrestling and Judo

Ray Takahashi comments: "Generally, wrestlers have a hard time making a transition to judo. Not only because of the differences in the sport but also because wrestlers rely too much on the physical and get frustrated with the preciseness required in the techniques of judo. Although they do well initially, at higher levels it catches up to them. And, for some reason they have difficulty refining technique to reach their true potential."

PROGRESSIVE STEPS FOR TECHNICAL TRAINING

The challenge lies in bridging the gap from learning a specific technique to being able to apply it in competition. Many judoka become frustrated when they have learned how to do a particular technique but find that they are unable to perform it in a dynamic resistive setting like competition. The spectrum from technique learning to competitive application is huge. This gap can only be bridged through specific training methods that initially must be followed in a progressive fashion as follows:

Stage 1: Technical Learning
- Learn a specific technique, its movements, actions, and body positioning.

Stage 2: Repetitions (Uchikomi)
- Replicate actions, focusing on proper technique.
- Develop speed and rhythm.
- Progress to moving uchikomi to develop timing and kuzushi (breaking opponent's balance).

Stage 3: Repetition in Dynamic Setting
- Execute the technique repetitively in a dynamic setting under controlled resistance to further develop timing, kuzushi, and movements (yakusoku-renshu).

Stage 4: Throwing Practice (Nage-Komi)
- Execute a throw in its entirety.

Stage 5: Dynamic Action Not Predetermined (Randori)

- Use minimal resistance.
- Use higher resistance.
- Use full resistance.

Note: You can practice situations where a certain part of a technique can be isolated. For example, practice the finishing phase of the throw by starting already in position (tsukuri phase). Depending on the resistance and the extent of the situation practiced, the drill can favor the tori (person practicing technique) or the uke (person technique is practiced on) once it becomes live.

Stage 6: Competition (Shiai)

- Perform the skill in a competitive environment.

As you develop and progress, the application of techniques in later stages should replicate closer and closer how you will perform them in competition. In particular, proper technical application is very important, so initial stages are no less important than later stages. Here are key applications you must master:

- When increasing speed of attack, ensure that the quality of the technique is not compromised.
- As you improve, variations and additional movements can be practiced, such as changing grips, angles, and positions of attack.
- Practice the throw using preliminary movements (tai-sabaki, kuzushi) and finish to its completion.
- Develop the ability to follow up and flow into other techniques or link into different situations.

UCHIKOMI TRAINING TO DEVELOP SPEED AND TECHNIQUE

Uchikomi can be described as drilling practice or repeating techniques over and over to develop speed and proper movements. The speed of repetitions can be altered depending on the objective. Numerous repetitions are possible because the focus is on the entry of the attack rather than the throwing action, allowing high numbers of repetitions. The main purpose of uchikomi is to acquire technical ability, although it can also serve as a specific physical-conditioning practice (to develop power and aerobic conditioning).

Uchikomi does not involve finishing the throw but rather only the kuzushi and tsukuri phases of the throw. Uchikomi training develops automation of the throw, so it is important to repeat the throws as correctly and identically as possible. Doing so will ensure you acquire the proper technique and your muscles follow the exact movements used in the technique. Practice your repetitions smoothly and rhythmically. Gradually, as you become more familiar with the technique, you can increase your speed and intensity and eventually replicate it as you would in competition. A well-trained judoka should be able to execute a repetition every second. Speed training will help power because speed is a component of power. So by training speed, you will also improve power.

The "10 and 10 rule" means it takes about 10 years of practice, or about 10,000 hours, to become proficient at a technique. Try writing your signature as fast as you can with your eyes closed. Years of training have allowed you to duplicate your signature so that it can be done fast and automatic. Now sign your name with your nondominant hand and compare. You can probably see that it takes a tremendous amount of practice to teach your body to move instinctively. The specific actions need to be learned by the body's nervous system and must then be practiced. The key is to perform the actions properly, so you must take special care in learning proper technique.

Uchikomi remains an integral training method for judo. Classical application of techniques is important for learning basic fundamental movements. Variations to techniques used in competition are sometimes difficult to reproduce. For example, some require certain resistances from your uke, which are difficult to repeat over and over to replicate a precise situation. In these cases, attempt to replicate situations where movement and resistances can be practiced together. Rather than practice only a static throw, therefore, create the dynamism of a match situation and perform the technique as you would in competition. This replication is necessary to make a link between the techniques practiced in the dojo and those applied in competition.

Following are five uchikomi drills along with photo illustrations.

Static Uchikomi

In static uchikomi, you attack from a static position (no preliminary movement).

a
At the start, break the grip.

b
Kuzushi plus entry.

c
Downward pull. Uke helps tori return to start position by pushing with the abdomen.

Shadow Uchikomi

This drill is valuable for improving footwork and quick body movements without a partner. Shadow uchikomi is analogous to the boxer who uses shadow boxing.

At the start, simulate kuzushi by tensing the muscles in the left arm.

Enter lightly and keep simulating kuzushi.

Simulate effort of the throw, using force to help return to the start position.

Power Uchikomi (Three Person)

Execute the repetition with greater power by continuing further into kake. The third person holds the uke from behind to keep him or her from being thrown.

The uke is reinforced from behind to take the throw.

The tori goes in and attempts to throw but is blocked by the uke and the helper behind the uke.

Alternating Uchikomi

This drill works on alternating the same or two different techniques that complement each other or attacking from one side and then the other. Alternating develops smooth transition between techniques. Both partners practice throws on each other.

a

Kuzushi plus entry.

b

Throwing effort plus resistance from uke.

c

Return to start position.

d

Kuzushi plus entry (left-side throw).

e

Tori is in position to throw plus resistance from uke.

Moving Uchikomi

Moving down a line while executing repetitions is an ideal way of developing timing and attacking on the move.

The tori pulls down, then up and back.

The tori slides back and pulls the uke's right arm across her face. Notice the uke has moved forward.

The tori steps back and pulls the uke's arms down then up.

The tori turns in and pulls. The uke is trying to stop his own forward motion.

Contact is made and the cycle is repeated.

NAGE-KOMI TRAINING FOR ACCURATE THROWS

Nage-komi is throwing practice in which the judoka repeats throws over and over, thus practicing the technique in its entirety. Throwing practice usually involves alternating throwing a number of partners a predetermined number of times. Nage-komi teaches the judoka to finish the throw entirely and make adjustments from partner to partner. One of the limitations to effective nage-komi is having the partners engage in such practice. Being thrown over and over again is taxing on the body; therefore, long durations of nage-komi are difficult for the uke.

Nage-komi is physically demanding for the tori as well, so it also serves as a good form of specific physical training. Maintaining proper technique even when you are tired is important because sloppy execution would likely be countered in an actual contest. You can lessen the degree of fatigue by altering how hard you execute the throws. Some throws are easier to execute than others depending on how much body movement is required. Hidetoshi Nakanishi, 1983 world champion, comments: "Before competitions I did huge numbers of nage-komi. In Japan, we have the great advantage of having many training partners, so nage-komi for 30 minutes is not a problem . . . except that it is exhausting" (*Seoi-Nage.* Hidetoshi Nakanishi. 1996. Ippon Books Ltd. England. Pg. 119).

Nage-komi should be preceded with proper kuzushi and preliminary movements so that timing can be developed. These movements might include moving while pulling with the arms to break the uke's balance in the direction of the throw. Once the uke's stance is disrupted, the judoka moves quickly into position and executes the throw. Attacking while moving is important because this kind of action occurs in randori and competition. Although the emphasis in nage-komi is on throwing, you can include setups, fakes, and combinations in your nage-komi practice (see chapter 9).

Hidetoshi Nakanishi, 1983 world champion, is well known for his work ethic and hard training. In this photo, taken in 2000, he runs the practice at Tokai University. Also with him are Ray Takahashi (center) and past world wrestling medalist for Japan, Noriaki Kiguchi (far right).

YAKUSOKU-RENSHU FOR COOPERATIVE PRACTICE

Yakusoku-renshu literally defined means "controlled or agreed-upon practice." It is characterized by cooperative practice of repetitively applying and receiving specific techniques that are agreed upon by each partner in advance. Yakusoku-renshu is an effective way to develop the rhythm and timing that is needed to execute the techniques in a dynamic setting. The judoka works with a uke on a predetermined technique and practices its application in a cooperative manner. Since both partners know what the other wants to do, they can cooperate by making openings or agreed-upon attacks (for counterattacks). And, because it is cooperative, no strength is required, and time and effort are not wasted. Both partners can practice pure technique in a safe, free-flowing manner.

RANDORI OR FREE PRACTICE

Randori is translated as "free practice." Free practice connotes that the judoka can do what he or she wants (that is, be free), but randori is nonetheless a deliberate method of judo training. Observing it, randori looks like contest fighting because it is dynamic, intense, and full of action. Randori allows you the opportunity to attack and defend freely in a dynamic setting.

In randori, avoid moving stiffly or robotically. Stiff movement is inadvisable for several reasons. One, it actually allows your opponent to know when and if you will attempt an attack (the movement is telegraphed easier). Second, being too stiff prevents you from developing the flow and rhythm that are necessary to attack in combination. Being too stiff also promotes defensive judo and does not allow you to explore and experiment with attack and defense. Last, stiff or robotic movement actually wastes energy, and you will tire faster than one who is able to relax the arms and body. It is better to avoid using too much strength by moving fluidly, which also develops better timing and rhythm.

A problem with physically strong judoka who have not developed good judo is an overemphasis on power, which is used to compensate for the lack of technique. Yasuhiro Yamashita distinguishes the use of power in randori, saying: "In building up your muscles (for example, weight training), it is not really necessary to 'release all your power.' The key point of randori is how to 'let loose your power' momentarily and achieve a state of kyo [emptiness]. If you can't do this, you will probably be criticized for being too stiff because of all that muscle training."

Practice Intensity

One of judo's greatest characteristics as a martial art is that randori can be practiced with high or full intensity. Intensity levels are different in some martial arts, where one cannot engage in all-out fighting because some techniques are dangerous; if applied fully there is an increased risk of injury. Martial arts that focused on striking and kicking were therefore relegated to practice with care and in structured forms or katas. Professor Kano realized this disadvantage in other martial arts in the formative years of judo, and he developed randori to simulate contestlike action safely.

It would be misleading to assume, however, that judo is totally risk free or "gentle" as the word "ju" defines it. Throwing and grappling on the ground is physically demanding, and in a one-on-one combative situation, randori can entail hard, rough fighting, especially if one is thrown hard to the mat or armlocked. It is this live action that makes randori realistic as it simulates real competition. Judoka enthusiasts find the intensity of randori very appealing. Randori should be practiced with varying speeds. Try to change the pace and speed of attack and defense so that it simulates what may happen in an actual match. Also, by practicing this way, you are prepared to change the tempo of the match if necessary in competition.

Practice a Winning Attitude

One of the goals of randori is to win. However, randori involves more than just trying to win. Beginners may think that winning is the only and ultimate goal because randori has a contestlike nature. In fact, the overall goal of randori is to "develop the ability to rapidly cope with changing circumstances, to build a strong and supple body, and to prepare mind and body for competition" (*Kodokan Judo*. Jigoro Kano. Ed. Kodokan Editorial Committee. Kodansha International. Tokyo. 1986. Pg. 142).

Many judoka often engage in randori with the wrong attitude and with the sole goal of wining the randori contest. It is known that winning can involve tactics, for example, stalling and holding on to the lead (see chapter 9). If the judoka holds on to the lead in randori by avoiding attack and exhibiting negative judo, randori is not being practiced to its fullest extent. Unfortunately, even advanced judoka practice randori with this win-driven attitude because of the overemphasis on competitive judo and a lack of overall understanding of the true goals of randori.

The Winning Perspective

Ray Takahashi notes that wrestlers who try judo have difficulty with the randori concept. In wrestling the similar free-practice training method is called "scrimmaging." In scrimmaging, however, the wrestling mind-set is different. One is taught to scrimmage for the win only and coached to never give up the point. Although this is also true in randori, in wrestling this goal guides the attitude of the activity. What many wrestlers do, therefore, is scrimmage to avoid being scored on and never open up to explore the dynamics of the activity. This prevents many secondary techniques from fully developing and ultimately will hinder true potential.

Practice Correct Posture

The posture in randori is shizen tai (natural posture). The judoka stands upright in a relaxed manner with the feet approximately shoulder-width apart. When the right foot is advanced the posture is migi (right) shizentai while a left advanced foot is called hidari (left) shizentai. Overly bent and defensive posture is discouraged. Shizentai is the best posture for efficient attack and defense. The focus is on standing judo (throwing). Standing judo (versus ground) allows for the greatest diversity of learning situations to occur. Timing, rhythm, and fundamental body movements (kuzushi, tai-sabaki) need to be emphasized. Use the necessary amount of strength, but do not overemphasize power. Success in attack and defense should not be a result of strength over technique. Engage in randori practice with ukes of different levels. Engage in randori with spirit.

Depending on the physical ability and experience level of your uke, you may consider approaching randori in different ways. If you both share similar ability and weight, then these conditions allow you both to fight to the maximum. However, if one of you has lesser ability, then the other should adjust the level down so the randori is equitable. This may involve focusing more on skill rather than strength, such as working on defensive evasions or combination techniques that require timing. If your uke is of higher ability, attempt to execute technique using sound fundamentals and maintaining good posture while attempting to attack as much as possible. Focusing on technique discourages overly defensive fighting that can lead to negative judo.

Regulate Resistance in Randori

Although randori can be performed with full resistance it is important to simulate the dynamic nature of randori without full intensity by regulating resistance in randori (RRR). The resistance between judoka is minimized so that more action and more techniques can be executed. The focus in RRR is on technical practice in a dynamic setting, yet it also serves as an important form of physical training. RRR links techniques, actions, setups, counters, and other movements to simulate randori training. By decreasing the resistance the judoka is able to work on more skills, such as secondary skills that would not work otherwise in randori. For example, let's say you want to practice the combination attack, ouchi-gari → seoi-nage. In a full-out randori session, you may be limited to performing the combination only a few times. This limitation is because against resistance, obtaining the proper reaction is more difficult so only a few attacks are possible. In a similar session with less resistance, you would be able to execute techniques easier. Because the understanding of RRR is technical, practice partners cooperate to provide realistic reactions with varying resistance. Because the activity is dynamic, you must still attack, make adjustments, react, and defend as you would in randori. The combination attack (ouchi-gari → seoi-nage) can then be executed with higher frequency and with greater success.

Fortunately in judo, the acceptance of RRR is more prevalent because of the philosophy of mutual welfare and benefit. The give-and-take and appreciation for one's training partner taught as part of judo practice enable the appreciation of RRR to be more fully developed.

Long sessions of RRR can be a good form of physical conditioning. By altering the intensity level (low to medium), you can control the work intensity over long periods. Medium- to high-intensity levels (maximum heart rate) are beneficial for developing aerobic stamina. The following are additional benefits of RRR:

- RRR can improve your aerobic conditioning, which helps in recovery between matches by training slow-twitch muscle fibers important for lactic-acid removal.

- RRR decreases your risk of injury because the intensity is lower.

- RRR increases the practice of attacks and defense situations (compared to randori) because you can engage in RRR for longer periods of time.

- RRR allows you to develop secondary techniques. Because intensity is low, you are able to have success in more situations and attacks.

- RRR teaches you to pace and regulate intensity more efficiently by working for long periods and altering resistance.

- RRR bridges the gap between uchikomi (singular technique) and randori (dynamic action).
- RRR helps you to develop flow and greater economical use of energy by forcing you to attack and defend without emphasizing strength.

KATA TRAINING FOR HIGHER LEVELS

Kata, or prearranged forms of exercises, was identified by Professor Kano as a training method for judo. Like jujitsu, from which it evolved, judo used kata as a training method for practicing techniques. The value of kata, however, and its practicality in competitive judo have often been debated. Many judoka fail to appreciate kata, and they often overlook its study. These judoka typically prefer to focus on competing and manage to advance in rank with little or no knowledge of kata.

There is no debate on the role of randori and related training methods (previously mentioned) for the competitive judoka. Considerable evidence also indicates that many successful competitive judoka have little to no kata training. And, many technical books directed toward the judo competitor fail to include kata as a training method. The connection between kata, the controlled practice of set patterns of movements depicting technique, is viewed as too far removed from what occurs in a dynamic, resistive setting such as a match. This fact is not to be refuted. But, the position taken in this book is to include kata as a worthy practice for the competitive judoka.

Kata is valuable because it provides a deep understanding of how techniques work. You must learn to interpret kata and implement the principles in your judo. As you develop in technical expertise, you will find that kata becomes more meaningful. Kata is not meant to replace other training methods, however; the competitive fighter should place a significant emphasis on randori and other training methods.

Judoka must understand two things about kata: Kata is limited, and its benefits are not direct in cause and effect. Kata depicts fundamental movements of attack and defense. Its structured sequences of techniques exemplify the principles of judo. Judoka wishing to advance their judo will engage in kata practice eventually, and it is usually included in grading requirements for the judoka once a senior belt level has been attained.

Most fighters know the importance of the development of a tokui-waza (favorite technique) to rely on, and this reliance is not to be denied. However, legendary fighter Masahiko Kimura, 8th Dan, said of kata: "Judo could become narrowed around one or two favorite techniques. Kata is important to experience the full scope of judo techniques." Kata practice provides a good balance in this regard. At the Takahashi Martial Arts School, a separate weekly class session devoted to kata learning and practice is not uncommon. June Takahashi, who was heavily influenced by Keiko Fukuda, 9th Dan, a kata specialist, says: "Kata is important for full judo learning. It provides meaning to technical study." Even top competitive judoka see the value of kata. Isao Inokuma (Olympic champion, 1964) said, "Kata taught me correct form for representative judo techniques. I applied it to improve my randori."

Some kata techniques represent situations that were derived from the beginnings of judo. Many kata have their basis in the days of the samurai and symbolize their movements. For example, in nage no kata, the sacrifice technique, uki-waza, symbolizes the engagement of two samurai warriors grasping each other on the battlefield. Without their swords they resort to hand-to-hand combat. As a more forceful samurai pushes, the other yields and makes use of the stronger opponent's force. The wide steps and over-and-under grip depicted in the kata represent the stance and movements of samurai dressed in full armor. The principles of judo—yielding, kuzushi, and the application of technique—are all reflected in this particular kata sequence.

Many judo fighters are attracted to kata only after their competitive careers when they can afford more time or when they need to fill the void of not competing. But, in effect, kata is competitive (there are kata tournaments), and the perfection of kata can cause one to be competitive with oneself in striving to be better at kata than one was the day before. The judoka is attempting to be as good as he or she can be, so there is a goal within kata practice to achieve and to improve as one would in competition. Using a sport analogy, golfers can appreciate the individual challenge of continually improving on their game.

Kata teaches "outer form," where the judoka must move with precision, authority, and flow. "You need to show spirit in kata," says June Takahashi, "Just movement of the techniques is not good enough." Isao Okano remarks, "As an instructor, I am always looking for new ideas to explain techniques and I use kata as a basic method of expression." It is said that kata is analogous to grammar in language. Once the rules of grammar are learned, techniques take on new meaning as the rules of grammar allow the development of sentences.

Kata practice is valuable for all judoka—the young, the elderly, men, and women. To begin training in kata, you should first start by studying it off the mat. That is, you should become familiar with the techniques, their order, and key points. Learning kata in conjunction with developing the techniques of judo is encouraged. Kata reinforces control and strengthens the movements and principles that make a technique work. For example, you can learn the throw, harai-goshi, as performed in nage no kata. Learning the sequence of movements would reinforce the yielding from a push, along with the application of kuzushi and the quick entry of the technique.

Harai-goshi can be practiced as demonstrated in kata. *(a)* Tori breaks uke's balance by pulling with the left hand. Tori's right hand is on the shoulder blade to maintain good contact. *(b)* Tori moves into position to thow with harai-goshi when uke's stance is off balance.

The following are benefits of learning kata:

- Learn the principles behind techniques and why they work
- Appreciate judo from the sport perspective
- Combine a technical focus with a mental focus
- Become a well-rounded judoka
- Build required aspects of judo for further progression, especially after a competitive career
- Experience a different form of performance through demonstration
- Enforce the spirit of judo

BLENDING KATA AND RANDORI

This section lists the main katas of the Kodokan as a complementary and balanced training method in combination with randori. Kata, which means "form," is a method of studying the fundamental principles of attack and defense in a prearranged system. The relationship of kata to randori is like grammar is to composition. Judoka interested in competing readily see the value of randori as a training method. As one advances to higher ranks, kata training and knowledge provides a fuller understanding of judo.

Nage No Kata: Forms of Throwing

This kata was developed to understand the theory of throwing techniques. There are five sets of three throwing techniques in nage no kata. Each set focuses on the main body part that is used and that makes the throw work. The first set of throws is classified as hand throws, followed by hip, leg, front-sacrificing, and side-sacrificing throws. Each throw is performed left and right. Table 4.1 details the techniques of nage no kata.

Katame No Kata: Forms of Grappling

Katame no kata promotes understanding the principles of the grappling techniques. Katame no kata is a set of prearranged forms of exercises consisting of five grappling techniques from each of the categories of hold-down, choking, and arm-lock techniques (see table 4.2).

Goshin-Jutsu: Forms of Self-Defense

Striking and self-defense techniques are not part of competitive judo because of the risk of injury. They are therefore only performed in kata. It is important to recognize that judo includes such techniques given the overemphasis of sport judo and consequently the lack of instruction and practice of overall judo technique. Goshin-jutsu shows modern techniques of self-defense consisting of grappling, throwing, empty-handed techniques, and techniques with weapons (see table 4.3).

Table 4.1—Nage No Kata: Formal Techniques of Throwing

Developed in 1884—teaches one to understand the theory of throwing techniques

			Uke	Tori
I. Te-waza—hand techniques				
1.	Uki-otoshi	Floating drop	Advancing right foot, take basic hold.	Turning body leftward 30°, drop left knee and pull uke straight down.
2.	Seoi-nage	Shoulder throw	Advancing with left foot, then right, strike top of tori's head with right fist.	Stepping in with right foot, block with left wrist; thrust right arm through uke's armpit; throw uke over shoulder.
3.	Kata-guruma	Shoulder wheel	Advancing right foot, take basic hold.	On second step, switch left grip to uke's inside sleeve; step back; turn 90°; assume jigotai; circle uke's right inner thigh with right arm; lift uke onto shoulders; throw uke to left front.
II. Koshi-waza—loin or hip techniques				
1.	Uki-goshi	Floating drop	Advance with left foot, then right; strike top of tori's head with right fist.	Step in obliquely with left foot, encircle uke's waist with left arm, grasp uke's sleeve with right hand and twist hips to the right to throw left uki-goshi.
2.	Harai-goshi	Hip sweep	Advancing right foot, take basic hold.	On the second tsugi-ashi, transfer right hand to uke's left shoulder blade; with right leg sweep uke's right leg upward.
3.	Tsurikomi-goshi	Lift-pull hip throw	Advancing right foot, take basic hold.	Grasp back of uke's collar, lift uke on second tsugi-ashi, step obliquely in front of uke's right foot on third step, pivot, and throw uke.
III. Ashi-waza—foot and leg techniques				
1.	Okuri-ashi-harai	Foot sweep	Uke and tori take basic hold.	Move with right tsugi-ashi, take a large third step, sweep uke's right outer ankle with left sole.
2.	Sasae-tsurikomi-ashi	Supporting foot lift-pull throw	Advancing right foot, take basic hold.	On the second step, slide right foot to right back corner; apply left sole to uke's advancing right ankle; pull down in large circular motion to left rear.
3.	Uchi-mata	Inner thigh reaping throw	Both take right natural posture and basic hold.	Move uke in a circular motion clockwise; on third step as uke is about to shift weight to left foot, thrust right leg between uke's legs; lift and throw, reaping uke's left thigh.

(continued)

Table 4.1 *(continued)*

			Uke	Tori
	**IV. Masutemi-waza—sacrifice throws on one's back**			
1.	Tomoe-nage	Circular throw	Both take right natural posture and basic hold.	Push uke backward by three steps, starting with right foot. When uke resists, switch left hand grip to lapel, place right foot on uke's abdomen, sit close to uke's left heel, straighten right leg, throw uke over the head.
2.	Ura-nage	Rear throw	Advancing with left foot, then right, strike top of tori's head with right fist.	Ducking the blow, step in with left foot; encircle uke's waist with left hand; place right foot between uke's feet; place right palm on uke's abdomen; fall back; throw uke over left shoulder.
3.	Sumi-gaeshi	Corner throw	Both engage in right jigotai, right hand on left shoulder blade and left hand on outer elbow.	Take large circular step back while lifting uke. Slide left foot close to the right foot, hook right instep behind uke's left knee, then fall back and throw uke over the head.
	**V. Yoko-sutemi-waza—sacrifice throws on one's side**			
1.	Yoko-gake	Side body drop	Both take right natural posture and basic hold.	Break uke's balance to right front corner; bring right foot beside left; fall to left, sweeping uke's right ankle with left sole.
2.	Yoko-guruma	Side wheel	Advancing with left foot, then right, strike top of tori's head with right fist.	Avoiding uke's blow, attempt ura-nage. Uke counters by bending forward, encircling neck with right arm. Fall on right side, thrust right leg between uke's legs, throw uke over left shoulder.
3.	Uki-waza	Floating throw	Both engage in right jigotai, right hand on left shoulder blade and left hand on outer elbow.	Take large circular step back, lifting uke forward; slide left foot to left side while lowering body to throw uke in a large arc over left shoulder.

Right-side executions must also be executed on the left.

Table 4.2—Katame No Kata: Formal Techniques of Grappling

Formulated in 1884—teaches theory and principles of ground techniques

			Tori	Uke
	**I. Osae-komi-waza—hold-down techniques**
1.	Kesa-gatame	Scarf hold	Trap uke's right arm under left arm, slide right hand under uke's armpit and put on left shoulder.	Clasp hands, lock tori's left elbow, twist, insert right knee between bodies, grasp tori's belt, bridge, try to throw tori over shoulder.
2.	Kata-gatame	Shoulder hold	Push uke's right elbow on cheek, slide right arm under uke's neck, clasp palms, right on top of left.	Clasp hands, push elbow up, twist to right, insert right knee under tori's hip, roll back over left shoulder.
3.	Kami-shiho-gatame	Top four-corner hold	Slide both hands under uke's shoulders and grip uke's belt; trapping uke's arms, press chest with chest; flatten feet.	Clasp hands together, wrap tori's neck, turn to side, insert left arm under tori's right armpit, twist, push tori's shoulders up with both hands, slip knees or feet between bodies.
4.	Yoko-shiho-gatame	Side locking four-corner hold	Pass right hand between uke's legs, insert right thumb in uke's belt, slide left hand under uke's neck and insert thumb in collar, turn uke's wrist clockwise, knees in, flatten feet.	Push tori's head back with left forearm, hook tori's head with left leg, twist, slip right knee under tori, grab back of tori's belt with left hand, push up tori's abdomen, roll tori forward to the left.
5.	Kuzure-kami-shiho-gatame	Broken top four-corner hold	Pass right hand under uke's right armpit; grasp back of uke's collar, thumb outside; slide left hand under uke's left shoulder; grasp uke's belt, thumb inside; press chest; knees in; flatten feet.	Insert left arm under tori's neck, hook neck with left leg, slip right knee under tori, twist to right, grab tori's belt with left hand and push up with right, bridge, try to lift tori leftward over head.
	**II. Shime-waza—neck hold lock**
1.	Kata-juji-jime	Half-cross lock	Press both of uke's carotid arteries, left thumb outside on left collar, right thumb inside on right; lean forward; pull up.	Push both of tori's elbows upward with both hands.
2.	Hadaka-jime	Naked lock	Place right wrist against uke's throat, clasp hands on uke's left shoulder, right cheek to left cheek, step back a pace.	Push tori's right arm up with both hands.
3.	Okuri-eri-jime	Sliding collar lock	Grasp uke's left lapel with right thumb base on left carotid, pull down uke's right lapel with left hand, right cheek on left cheek, press back of uke's neck with right shoulder, twist to the right.	Seize tori's upper sleeve with right hand, elbow section with left hand, pull downward with hands.

(continued)

Table 4.2 (continued)

			Tori	**Uke**
4.	Kata ha-jime	Single-wing lock	Grasp uke's left lapel with right thumb base on left carotid, with left arm lift uke's left arm straight up, insert left palm on nape of uke's neck, shift right foot to right.	Seize own left wrist, lifting left arm.
5.	Gyaku-juji-jime	Reverse cross lock	Four fingers outside, apply pressure on uke's carotid with thumb base of both hands, pull uke's neck toward chest.	Push tori's left elbow from above with right hand and right elbow from below with left hand.
III. Kansetsu-waza—joint techniques				
1.	Ude-garami	Entangled armlock	With left hand thumb down take uke's left wrist and press down near shoulder, insert right hand under uke's elbow, grasp own wrist from the top, pull uke's wrist towards left shoulder joint, raising uke's elbow.	Unable to escape, tap twice.
2.	Ude-hishigi-juji-gatame	Cross armlock	Take uke's right wrist with both hands, right above the left; pull up, placing right foot into uke's right armpit; swing left foot counterclockwise over uke's head, placing sole of foot on mat near uke's shoulder; trap uke's arm; lie down; bring knees together; raise hips.	Bend right arm toward right shoulder joint, roll leftward.
3.	Ude-hishigi-ude-gatame	Arm armlock	Trap uke's left wrist between neck and right shoulder; place palm of right hand on uke's left elbow, left hand over the right; twist uks's arm to left and up; press uke's arm toward chest.	Pull left arm downward, twisting body rightward.
4.	Ude-hishigi-hiza-gatame	Knee armlock	From basic hold, release grip from left sleeve, transfer it counter-clockwise to outer sleeve, trap uke's right wrist under armpit. Put toes of right foot on uke's left hip joint and fall to right, placing left foot on uke's right hip; place knee on own left hand to apply pressure to uke's elbow.	Pull left arm free.
5.	Ashi-garami	Entangled leg lock	From basic hold, attempt right tomoe-nage. Uke steps forward and lifts up. Push inside of uke's left knee with right foot, hook left leg over uke's right leg, wedge left foot against right lower abdomen, twist hip to right, straighten left leg, pull with both hands.	Twist to left.

Table 4.3—Kodokan Goshin-Jutsu: Kodokan Self-Defense Forms

Developed in 1956—designed for self-defense techniques against forms of unarmed or armed attacks.

			Uke	Tori
I. Against unarmed attack				
i. When held				
1.	Ryote-dori	Two-hand hold	Step in left foot, grasp both of tori's wrists, kick tori's groin with right knee.	Release right wrist, strike uke's right temple with knife edge of hand, kote-hineri, press elbow.
2.	Hidari-eri-dori	Left-lapel hold	Step forward with right foot, grasp tori's left lapel and push.	Strike uke's eyes with back of hand; with right hand, grab uke's right wrist; twist uke's wrist and push the elbow to mat with left hand; left knee on uke's back.
3.	Migi-eri-dori	Right-lapel hold	Pull down tori's right lapel, step back on left foot.	Uppercut with right fist, grab uke's right wrist to chest and throw, kote-gaeshi.
4.	Kataude-dori	Single-hand hold	From right rear grab tori's right wrist with right hand and tori's elbow with the left hand.	Kick left side of uke's left knee with sole of right foot, apply waki-gatame to uke's right arm
5.	Ushiro-eri-jime	Collar hold from behind	From behind, pull down back of tori's collar; step back on left foot.	Protecting face, punch uke's solar plexus with right hand; apply left ude-gatame to right arm.
6.	Ushiro-jime	Choke from behind	Apply right hadaka-jime over right shoulder.	Pull uke's arm down, slip head free; grip uke's right wrist with left hand, apply te-gatame to uke's right elbow.
7.	Kakae-dori	Seize and hold from behind	Step forward with right foot and embrace tori in a bear hug.	Stomp uke's right foot, turn, grasp uke's right wrist with left hand, lock right elbow with arm, throw uke forward.
ii. At a distance				
1.	Naname-uchi	Slanting strike	Step forward with right foot, blow to tori's left temple with right fist.	Parry right arm with left, uppercut with right arm; grab uke's throat, then throw uke with right osoto-gari.
2.	Ago-tsuki	Uppercut	Step forward with right foot, uppercut to tori's chin with right fist.	With right hand, deflect blow; grab and twist uke's wrist toward his or her shoulder; throw uke forward.
3.	Ganmen-tsuki	Thrust-punch face	Step forward with left foot, punch tori's face with left fist.	Step forward with right foot, punch uke's side with right fist, apply hadaka-jime from behind.

(continued)

Table 4.3 (continued)

			Uke	Tori
4.	Mae-geri	Front kick	Step forward with left foot, kick tori's groin with right sole of foot.	Step back on right foot, scoop uke's ankle and push back.
5.	Yoko-geri	Side kick	Step to left front corner with left foot, kick tori's right side with right foot.	Step to left front corner, parry with right forearm, move behind uke, pull down uke's shoulders.

<table>
<tr><td colspan="5" align="center">II. Against armed attack</td></tr>
</table>

i. Dagger

			Uke	Tori
1.	Tsukkake	Thrust	Step back on right foot, withdraw dagger and hold it at tori's right side.	Step to right, take left elbow with right hand, blind uke's eyes with left palm, grab uke's left wrist with left hand, push uke's elbow to mat, apply te-gatame.
2.	Choku-zuki	Straight thrust	Step forward with left foot; from right waist, thrust dagger to tori's stomach.	Step to the left, turn, grab uke's right elbow with left hand, uppercut, apply right waki-gatame.
3.	Naname-zuki	Slanting stab	Step forward with left foot, stab right side of tori's neck while stepping in with right foot.	Step back with right foot, grab uke's wrist, throw uke with kote-gaeshi, apply te-gatame, take dagger.

ii. Stick

			Uke	Tori
1.	Furi-age	Upswing against stick	Step back with right foot, swing stick upward over head.	Step in with left foot, block uke's right arm, push uke's chin up with right hand, throw uke with right osoto-gari.
2.	Furi-oroshi	Downswing against stick	Step forward with right foot, strike left side of tori's head.	Step back right foot, step forward on left; hit uke's face with side of left fist, then hit with te-gatana.
3.	Morote-zuki	Two-hand thrust against stick	Step forward with left foot, thrust stick to tori's solar plexus.	Deflect stick with right hand; grab end with left hand, grab between uke's hands with right; pressing left elbow, throw to uke's right.

iii. Pistol

			Uke	Tori
1.	Shomen-zuki	Pistol at the abdomen	Step forward with right foot, press pistol against tori's abdomen.	Raise hands; grab uke's pistol with left hand, grab uke's right wrist with right hand; push barrel to uke's right armpit.
2.	Koshi-gamae	Pistol held at the side	Step forward with left foot pointing at tori's abdomen.	Twist to left, grab barrel top with right hand and bottom with left, twist to right, pull, hit uke's head.
3.	Haimen-zuki	Pistol against the back	Hold pistol in middle of tori's back.	Raise hands, turn right, wrap right arm around uke's right arm, take gun away with left hand.

OTHER KATA IN JUDO

Judo includes other kata that are listed in this section. The judoka may not engage in all forms of kata but should be informed about what they are.

Seiryoku Zen'Yo Kokumin Taiiku: Maximum-Efficiency National Physical Education Forms

Seiryoku zen'yo kokumin taiiku is a set of Kodokan formal exercises devised as a means of general physical education based on the principle of maximum efficiency. It comprises solo striking movements and portions of paired movements adapted from the kime no kata and ju no kata. See table 4.4.

Left front cross blow. Step to your left front corner with your right foot and punch.

Right-side blow. Bring fist back to left shoulder and strike to the right while stepping to the side.

Large rear strike. Drop your right arm to your side and unclench your fist. Step back with your right foot and strike to the rear with the elbow.

Large front blow. Step forward with your right foot and punch to the front.

Large upward blow. Bring your feet back to the original position, bend your knees and rise to punch straight up.

Table 4.4—Seiryoku Zen'yo Kokumin Taiiku: Maximum Efficiency National Physical Education Kata

Promotes the development of strong, healthy minds and bodies.

		I. Tandoku-renshu—individual exercises	
1.		Goho-ate	Five-directional strike
	1.	Hidari-mae-naname-ate	Left-front crossing blow
	2.	Migi-ate	Right-side blow
	3.	Ushiro-ate	Rear strike
	4.	Mae-ate	Front blow
	5.	Ue-ate	Upward blow
2.		Ogoho-ate	Large five-directional strike
	1.	Ohidari-mae-naname-ate	Large left-front crossing blow
	2.	Omigi-ate	Large right-side blow
	3.	Oushiro-ate	Large rear strike
	4.	Omae-ate	Large front blow
	5.	Oue-ate	Large upward blow
3.		Goho-geri	Five-directional kick
	1.	Mae-geri	Front kick
	2.	Ushiro-geri	Rear kick
	3.	Hidari-mae-naname-geri	Left-front crossing kick
	4.	Migi-mae-naname- geri	Right-front crossing kick
	5.	Taka-geri	High front kick
4.		Kagami-migaki	Mirror polishing
		The mirror represents the human mind, the act of polishing represents the ethics by which our minds are defined.	
5.		Sayu-uchi	Strike to both sides
6.		Zengo-tsuki	Front rear strike
7.		Ryote-ue-tsuki	Two-hand upward blow
8.		Oryote-ue-tsuki	Large two-hand upward blow
9.		Sayu-kogo-shita-tsuki	Left-right downward strike
10.		Ryote-shita-tsuki	Two-hand downward blow
11.		Naname-ue-uchi	Front-side upward cut
12.		Naname-shita-uchi	Front-side downward cut
13.		Onaname-ue-uchi	Large slanting upward cut
14.		Usihro-sumi-tsuki	Rear corner blow
15.		Ushiro-uchi	Rear blow
16.		Ushiro-tsuki, mae-shita-tsuki	Rear downward blow

II. Sotai-renshu—joint exercises			
1. Kime shiki			**Forms of decision**
i.	Idori		Kneeling techniques
	1.	Ryote-dori	Two-hand hold
	2.	Furihanashi	Shaking loose
	3.	Gyakute-dori	Reverse two-hand hold
	4.	Tsukkake	Stomach punch
	5.	Kiri-gake	Head cut
ii.	Tachiai		Standing techniques
	1.	Tsuki-age	Uppercut
	2.	Yoko-uchi	Side blow
	3.	Ushiro-dori	Hold from behind
	4.	Naname-tsuki	Carotid cut
	5.	Kiri-oroshi	Downward cut

Kime No Kata: Decisive Technique Forms

Kime no kata was designed to teach fundamental ways and means of defending against attacks using throwing, grappling, and striking techniques. These techniques are performed in a kneeling position and in a standing position. Kime no kata is also known as shinken shobu no kata (forms of combat). See table 4.5.

Itsutsu No Kata: The Five Forms

Itsutsu no kata is a set of five techniques, known only by their number, expressing principles of attack and defense in movements evocative of natural phenomenon such as relating to abstract concepts like water and wind. They are considered to be expressions of the artistry of judo (*Kodokan New Japanese-English Dictionary of Judo*. Teizo Kawamura and Toshiro Daigo. 2000. Kodokan Judo Institute. Tokyo. Pg. 79). See table 4.6.

Koshiki No Kata: Classical or Antique Forms

Koshiki no kata was based upon the Kito Ryu School of Jujitsu from which modern judo techniques were derived and illustrates techniques while wearing armor. Professor Kano revised and adapted these forms to show the substance of judo. See table 4.7.

Ju No Kata: Forms of Gentleness and Flexibility

Ju no kata shows ways of attack and defense through arranged gentle and expressive movements that exemplify the principles of judo. See table 4.8.

As you have seen, mastery of judo's varied training methods is critical to the competitive judoka. To apply the methods learned in this chapter turn to chapter 5, "Breakfalls, Posture, and Standing and Ground Positions."

Table 4.5—Kime No Kata: Forms of Decision

Formulated in 1888—teaches efficient techniques of attack and defense in combat situations

			Uke	Tori
I. Idori—kneeling posture				
i. Attacks with bare hand				
1.	Ryote-dori	Two-hand hold	On toes, seize both of tori's wrists.	Kick uke's solar plexus with right foot, waki-gatame to uke's left arm.
2.	Tsukkake	Stomach punch	On toes, punch tori's solar plexus with right fist.	Punch between uke's eyes, apply choke and hara-gatame to uke's right elbow.
3.	Suri-age	Forehead thrust	On toes, thrust right palm to tori's forehead.	Kick uke's solar plexus with right foot, ude-gatame on uke's right arm with left knee.
4.	Yoko-uchi	Side blow	On toes, strike tori's left temple with fist.	Duck, push down, apply kata-gatame, strike uke's solar plexus with right elbow.
5.	Ushiro-dori	Hold from behind	Raise right knee, embrace tori's upper body with both hands.	Roll to left with ippon-seoi-nage into ushiro-kesa, punch uke's groin with left fist.
ii. Attacks with dagger				
1.	Tsukkomi	Dagger thrust to stomach	On toes, step forward on left foot; stab tori's solar plexus.	Strike between uke's eyes with right fist, choke and hara-gatame to uke's right arm.
2.	Kiri-komi	Downward slash	On toes, step forward on right foot; slap top of tori's head.	Catch uke's wrist with both hands, waki-gatame to uke's right arm.
3.	Yoko-tsuki	Dagger thrust to side	On toes, turn left foot 90°; thrust dagger to tori's right side.	Deflect uke's elbow, punch between uke's eyes, choke and hara-gatame on uke's right arm.

			Uke	Tori
II. Tachiai—standing posture				
i. Attacks with bare hand				
1.	Ryote-dori	Two-hand hold	Step forward on right foot, seize both of tori's hands.	Kick uke's groin with right foot, waki-gatame on uke's left arm.
2.	Sode-tori	Sleeve grab	Take tori's left sleeve, push with right hand, right foot forward.	Kick uke's right knee with left foot, pivot 180°, right osoto-gari.
3.	Tsukkake	Punch to face	Fake left punch, punch between tori's eyes with right fist.	Parry uke's right arm, step behind uke, hadaka-jime with right hand.
4.	Tsuki-age	Uppercut	Right foot forward, right uppercut to tori's chin.	Take uke's wrist up with both hands, waki-gatame to uke's right arm.
5.	Suri-age	Forehead thrust	Strike tori's forehead with right palm, right foot forward.	Parry uke's blow, punch uke's solar plexus with right fist, left uki-goshi.
6.	Yoko-uchi	Side blow	Strike tori's left temple with right fist, right foot forward.	Bend forward, avoiding uke's blow; step behind uke; okuri-eri-jime.
7.	Keage	Groin kick	Step forward on left foot, kick tori's groin with ball of right sole.	Step back with right foot, catch uke's ankle with both hands, kick uke's groin with right foot.
8.	Ushiro-dori	Hold from behind	Take a large step with right foot, embrace tori's upper body.	Right seoi-nage, strike between uke's eyes with te-gatana.
ii. Attacks with dagger or sword				
1.	Tsukkomi	Dagger thrust to stomach	Step forward with left foot, stab tori's stomach with right hand.	Punch between uke's eyes with right fist, choke, hara-gatame.
2.	Kiri-komi	Downward slash	Step forward on right foot, slash top of tori's head.	Catch uke's wrist, choke and waki-gatame to uke's right arm.
3.	Nuki-kake	Sword unsheathing	Step forward on right foot, attempt to unsheath sword.	Seize uke's right wrist with right hand, step to rear, kata ha-jime.
4.	Kiri-oroshi	Downward cut	Right foot forward, slash top of tori's head.	Step to left front to dodge uke's blow, right hand on uke's wrist, choke and hara-gatame to uke's right arm.

Table 4.6—Itsutso No Kata: The Five Forms

Originated in the Tenjinshinyo Jujitsu School—included as Kodokan kata in 1997. Demonstrates the principle of maximum efficiency. The graceful movements are evocative of the motion of water, the heavenly bodies, and other natural forces.

Forms				Interpretation
I.	Oshi-kaeshi	Continuous pushing	Uke pushes on tori's chest with palm alternating thumb side first, then little finger side.	Continuous attack will defeat a strong power.
II.	Eige	Draw prop	Uke lunges forward to stab tori's abdomen with right hand.	Energy of opponent's attack is used to defeat him or her.
III.	Tomo-wakare	Separation	Both circle around each other like Chinese phoenixes.	Inner circle of whirlpool controls outer circle.
IV.	Roin	Pulling tide	Swing arms back to the left as if casting a net.	Everything on shore is drawn back into the ocean by the power of the tide.
V.	Sekka no wakare	Instant separation	Both raise arms like Chinese phoenixes.	When energies collide, one yields to avert destroying both.

Table 4.7—Koshiki No Kata: Forms Antique

Originated in the Kito School of Jujitsu—kata designed for samurai warriors in armor. Embodies the principles and techniques of Kodokan judo.

	Omote	**Front**
1.	Tai	Ready posture
2.	Yume-no-uchi	Dreaming
3.	Ryokuhi	Strength dodging
4.	Mizu-guruma	Water wheel
5.	Mizu-nagare	Water flow
6.	Hikiotoshi	Draw drop
7.	Ko-daore	Log fall
8.	Uchikudaki	Smashing
9.	Tani-otoshi	Valley drop
10.	Kuruma-daore	Wheel throw
11.	Shikoro-dori	Grabbing the neck plates
12.	Shikoro-gaeshi	Twisting the neck plates
13.	Yudachi	Shower
14.	Taki-otoshi	Waterfall drop
	Ura	**Rear**
1.	Mi-kudaki	Body smashing
2.	Kuruma-gaeshi	Wheel throw
3.	Mizu-iri	Water plunge
4.	Ryusetsu	Willow snow
5.	Sakaotoshi	Headlong fall
6.	Yukiore	Snowbreak
7.	Iwa-nami	Wave on the rocks

Table 4.8—Ju No Kata: Forms of Gentleness

Formulated in 1887—teaches offensive and defensive methods by the principles of ju

			Uke	Tori
Ikkyo—set I				
1.	Tsuki-dashi	Hand thrust	Advance right tsugi-ashi, thrust right fingers between tori's eyes.	Tori and uke escape by turning 180° twice; with left palm on left shoulder, raise uke's right hand backward.
2.	Kata-oshi	Shoulder push	Push tori's right shoulder forward.	Bend; stepping back, grasp uke's right hand; catch uke's left hand as uke attacks between eyes; pull both of uke's arms straight up and backward.
3.	Ryote-dori	Seizure of two hands	Grasp both of tori's wrists.	Release uke's right hand, grasp uke's right elbow, lift as makikomi.
4.	Kata-mawashi	Shoulder turn	Turn tori, push tori's right shoulder, pull tori's left front shoulder.	With left hand, grasp uke's right elbow from inside; right palm on uke's right shoulder; lift as ippon-seoi-nage.
5.	Ago-oshi	Jaw push	Advance right tsugi-ashi, push and turn tori's jaw.	Seize uke's palm, pull and turn palm 180°; catch uke's left attacking hand; pull both of uke's arms upwards and back, then down to shoulders.
Nikkyo—set II				
1.	Kiri-oroshi	Downward cut	Pivot 90° right, stretch up right hand, cut down on tori's head with knife edge.	With right hand, catch uke's wrist; as uke pushes elbow, turn; take uke's left hand, pull up and back, right hand on uke's left shoulder.
2.	Ryokata-oshi	Two-shoulder push	Left sides to kamiza, tori in front, push down on both of tori's shoulders.	Bend knees; pivot 360°; taking uke's right wrist, step forward pulling up; press uke's left hand across chest as tani-otoshi.
3.	Naname-uchi	Slanting strike	Strike between tori's eyes with knife edge of right hand.	Block with left hand, slanting strike to uke's forehead with right hand, uke pulls, tori turns, step right foot behind lift as ura-nage.

			Uke	**Tori**
4.	Katate-dori	One-hand hold	Facing kamiza, grasp tori's right wrist with left hand.	Bend elbow, release grip, turning to uke's push, encircle uke's waist; lift as left uki-goshi.
5.	Katate-age	One-hand lift	Uke and tori raise right arms, stepping forward with small steps almost colliding.	Withdraw right foot 90°, control uke's right elbow down to the right, then up to the left; pull uke's wrist up and backward, left hand on uke's left shoulder.

Sankyo—set III

			Uke	**Tori**
1.	Obi-tori	Belt seizure	Step foward with left foot, left hand crossed over right, palm down.	Grasp uke's left wrist with right hand, elbow with left; uke takes right elbow; both left sides facing kamiza; encircle uke's waist with left arm; lift as uki-goshi.
2.	Mune-oshi	Chest push	With right hand, push tori's left chest.	Tori and uke deflect and counterattack, both turning each other; grip uke's right wrist with left hand slanted downward; control uke's left elbow; step behind uke's right foot.
3.	Tsuki-age	Uppercut	Step back on right foot, raise right outstretched hand from rear, clench fist, step in with right foot, uppercut to tori's chin.	Catch uke's fist with right hand; push uke's elbow; stepping left foot forward, turning uke 180°, step right foot behind uke; push uke's right arm up; apply ude-garami.
4.	Uchi-oroshi	Downward strike	Raise right hand in circle, fingers stretched; clench fist; strike tori's head, step in with right foot.	As in kiri-oroshi, uke and tori turn each other; with left hand, grasp uke's left wrist, right wrist on uke's throat in hadaka-jime.
5.	Ryogan-tsuki	Strike to both eyes	Step in with right foot, poke tori's eyes with right middle and ring finger.	Escaping and defending, uke and tori counterattack each other; tori pokes uke's eyes with left hand; tori lifts as uki-goshi.

Breakfalls, Posture, and Standing and Ground Positions

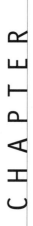

Even the advanced judoka should not overlook the fundamental positions and skills of judo. Many basic positions and skills lead to higher levels of learning, and there are many instances where the basics emerge as determinants of success, even at the highest levels of competition. A solid acquisition of breakfalls, posture, and fundamental standing and ground positions should precede acquisition of all other techniques in judo. For best overall judo learning, develop your standing judo first followed by specializing on the ground.

A review of the fundamentals is also important to those who have some experience because they may have developed bad habits that need to be broken. Even judoka with considerable experience such as elite fighters often overlook the fundamentals, which can hinder further progress. If nothing else, a review further reinforces the practice and study of essential skills and techniques.

BREAKFALLS: UKEMI

Breakfalls (front rolling, back, side, front) are considered the most important skill, and their importance is reflected every time you are thrown to the mat. The principle of why they work is the distribution of force, or impact of the body landing on the mat over a large surface area. For example, if you land on one body part (elbow), all the force of the fall is directed into that body part, which can lead to injury such as, in the worst possible case, a shoulder separation. By spreading the impact of a fall over a larger body surface (for example, the arms, legs, and back) the force is decreased, thereby decreasing risk of injury.

Safety is of prime importance in judo, and you must learn how to breakfall with confidence. Once you know how to breakfall correctly, you appreciate judo even more because breakfalls allow you to engage in throwing practice and randori without the fear of falling. If you are afraid to fall, you are not able to engage in judo to its fullest. Depending on the type of technique by which one is thrown, four main types of breakfalls are used: front rolling, forward falling, side, and backward.

Allyn Takahashi throws his opponent. Knowing how to breakfall correctly reduces the risk of injury.

Front-Rolling Breakfall: Zenpo Kaiten

In this example, the opponent is thrown by seoi-nage or other front-bending rotational throws.

Roll over (to either your left or right side) in a somersault action: From a right-leg lead, initiate a forward somersault action, tucking your head in while rolling over. Make sure that a right-leg lead results in slapping your left hand and vice versa.

Next, contact the mat simultaneously with your legs, hands, and body—landing on your side. As your body comes around to land, synchronize your legs and arms to hit the mat flat. Land on your side, feet apart, knees flexed, head up, and slapping hand flat to the mat, protecting your spine and head.

Right-leg and right-hand lead. Notice the smooth, round motions.

Left hand slaps the mat. Notice the legs are not crossed.

Forward-Falling Breakfall: Mae Ukemi

In this example, the opponent is thrown to a prone position (facedown). Although throws are not meant to land the person in a prone position, in rare situations a facedown landing may occur, particularly when the uke attempts to defend.

Fall so that your forearms contact the mat on landing (taking the force): Keep your hands up, palms facing the mat. Prepare to hit the mat by tensing your body and keeping your arms forward.

Your hands should be turned inward about 45 degrees so that your elbows bend outward. Slap the mat hard while looking away to one side. Contact the mat as flat as possible over your entire forearm.

Falling forward when a side breakfall or rolling breakfall is not possible.

Be careful not to land directly on your elbows. Also avoid hitting the mat with your abdomen and lower body. All of the force should be received in your palms and forearms.

Side Breakfall: *Yoko Ukemi*

In this example, the opponent is thrown by a okuri-ashi-barai.

When thrown sideways as in okuri-ashi-barai, your feet do not always land simultaneously with your body. Depending on how you are thrown, you may be required to perform a side breakfall, where your body and slapping hand contact the mat before your legs. As you begin to make contact with the mat, prepare to slap it at the same time your upper body lands.

The uke is thrown sideways. The tori has released the uke's left arm and is pulling upwards with both hands to help the uke break the fall.

Step forward with the left foot and advance the right foot as if swept out by a foot sweep. Allow the foot to continue upward, following through with the right arm while falling sideways.

The right arm slaps the mat, the feet are up and together.

Lower your body by bending your support leg. Fall sideways and slap your mat hand as your upper body contacts the mat. As you fall sideways in a pike position (bent at the waist), your body and your slapping arm contact the mat before your legs.

Keep your feet together and roll vertically on contact. Hit the mat hard while rolling into the side-breakfall position. When rolling into the fall, carry your legs so they point straight upward.

Backward Breakfall: Koho Ukemi

In this example, the opponent is thrown straight backward (morote-gari or double-leg tackle). When you are thrown straight backward, execute a back breakfall. Keep your head up to prevent your head from hitting the mat.

To practice the backward breakfall, start in the sitting or standing position with your arms extended horizontally in front. As you fall backward keeping a pike position, your arms slap the mat approximately 30 to 45 degrees from your body. Tense your neck so your head is kept in the flexed position to prevent it from contacting the mat. As your back contacts the mat, simultaneously hit with your arms at approximately 30- to 45-degree angles from your body. Keep your body tense on contact with the mat.

Notice the head is raised, the chin is tucked in, and the arms are slapping the mat approximately 30 degrees from the body.

Fall backward keeping your head forward.

Slap your arms to the mat as your upper body makes contact.

POSTURE

Good posture in judo enables you to move freely to attack and defend effectively. Good posture is also expected in competition. Overly defensive posture is frowned on and, if prolonged, can result in a penalty because it does little to contribute to the spirit of judo.

At the start of a match many judoka exhibit an upright posture by outstretching their arms to show a dominant stance to their opponent. Such posture demonstrates confidence and shows that they are ready to fight.

To assume good general posture, take a natural standing position with your feet slightly wider than shoulder-width apart. Shift your body weight forward slightly so that more weight is taken by the front of your feet. This allows you to move quickly and not be caught flat-footed. This basic natural posture is called shizen hontai.

By advancing either leg, one can take a right or left basic natural posture. In competition, many fighters emphasize one side depending on how strong or balanced they are in attack and defense. For example, boxers either take a right- or left-handed stance (south paw) depending on what hand delivers their power punch. Judo fighters develop techniques to complement their arsenal of attacks and lead a leg accordingly.

Natural standing posture (shizen hontai). Feet are shoulder-width apart. Keep the body position straight, upright, and relaxed.

Advanced leg, right natural posture (migi shizentai). From natural posture, advance one foot slightly (right or left, often depending on which is dominant). Posture is straight and upright and weight is distributed evenly on both feet.

In a competitive situation the judoka alters or moves out of shizen hontai, especially when in a defensive situation. The basic defensive posture is called jigo hontai. Spread your feet wide apart and lower your stance (bend at the knees) to achieve greater stability.

Again, by advancing either leg, you can take a right or left basic defensive posture. Good posture and proper grip permits you to move easily and perform basic movements. (For more on gripping, see chapter 6.)

Phil Takahashi engages in natural posture with the left leg advanced (hidari shizen hontai). His opponent is Jean-Pierre Cantin, nine-time Canadian Senior National champion and national coach.

FOOTWORK

You must be able to stay light on your feet so that you can perform movements quickly. Inexperienced or beginner judoka often move awkwardly because they move with the same principles as those of regular walking. Beginners who are too stiff look robotic and inefficient in their use of strength (they tend to use too much). Do not walk in judo practice in a pedestrian fashion (like walking down the street), in which your body weight is shifted over one leg and then the next as you take a step. Pedestrian walking makes you vulnerable to attack (all your weight is on one leg). Instead, move by always leading with one foot and moving the other foot up to meet the first. After each step, assume good position (for example, shizen hontai). This way the shift of your body weight is minimized and you are able to move quickly in all directions—forward, backward, sideways, and diagonally (called tsugi-ashi or shuffle stepping).

Footwork in judo is important to maintain balance. It allows you to attack and defend. *(a* and *b)* Forward tsugi-ashi is performed by stepping forward with one foot then moving the other foot up to meet it, then moving the first foot again. Slide your feet across the mat and keep your weight forward off your heels. *(c* and *d)* Side tsugi-ashi repeats similar stepping actions but is performed sideways. Move sideways by stepping with one leg followed by the next. Always slide your feet across the mat and keep your weight forward on the front of your feet. Do not bounce or overly raise your body up and down while moving.

THROWING MECHANICS

The ability to move your body in a controlled manner and make turns (tai-sabaki, quarter and half pivots, half steps) are key elements in creating kuzushi, which is a main component of executing throws. These movements and the ability of using your opponent's momentum and force exemplify the essence of throwing in judo. Once you have broken your opponent's balance, you can apply a technique (seoi-nage).

Kuzushi

The action of throwing can often be broken down into three phases: kuzushi, tsu-kuri, and kake. In the initial phase, kuzushi is important when entering the throw where the critical point is to disrupt your opponent's balance. Kuzushi allows you to attack when your opponent is vulnerable. It can be difficult to move an opponent off balance, especially if your opponent is resisting as in a match setting. Sometimes a hard pull of the arms is insufficient to disrupt your opponent's stance. The ability to move (tai-sabaki) assists kuzushi, and perfecting the timing of when to apply strength requires considerable practice. For example, if you aim to attack backward with ouchi-gari, you need to execute a push to disrupt your opponent's balance backward. Let's say the push needed is equal to a force of 10 pounds. Now, if you precede your attack with a forward fake (for example, seoi-nage) and your opponent reacts by pulling backward (4 pounds), you can utilize this overcompensation with your intended ouchi-gari attack. The net result would be 6 pounds of force needed, rather than 10 pounds.

Pull uke's sleeve upwards, turning the left hand so little finger is up and palm faces outward. Drive fist upwards to lift uke's weight off his heel.

Continue pulling forward and with the knees bent, turn and contact uke below his center of gravity to throw him.

Tsukuri: Contact, Positioning, and Setup

In the tsukuri phase of throwing, position your body quickly so that conditions are ready for throwing. For example, in seoi-nage you would move your feet into position, bend your knees so that your hips contact below your opponent's hips, and make contact with your back to the uke's chest. This phase is difficult because you need to position your body quickly before the kuzushi phase is lost. This phase is analogous to the sprinter who holds the "set" position in the starting blocks. All your muscles are tensed and ready to contract, like a compressed spring ready to release. When you position in tsukuri (seoi-nage), you will want to follow quickly into kake, or throwing.

The tsukuri phase of throwing involves setting up and positioning the body to make contact. Once you have broken the uke's balance, move into position quickly to ensure good contact. Usually, holding this position is difficult because all your muscles are tensed and ready to contract into the throwing phase.

Kake: Throwing or Finishing

In kake, the final phase, you finish the throw. If you executed the preceding two phases well, you should be able to follow through with kake relatively easily. Contract your muscles and follow through with good balance for a proper finish. In the case of seoi-nage, pull down with your arms and extend your legs (ankles, knees, hip) so that your opponent rotates around during the throwing action.

During kake, or throwing phase, contract your muscles and follow through to execute the throw.

Ray Takahashi executes a low ippon-seoi-nage. Ray will need a strong kake, or finish, to throw his opponent over.

GROUND MOVEMENTS AND POSITIONS

The three main ways to win on the ground using grappling techniques include hold-downs, armlocks, and chokes. The offensive judoka attempts to win in these ways by scoring ippon. Only in hold-downs are partial scores (koka, yuko, waza-ari) awarded in addition to ippon. Therefore, a choke or armlock that does not make the opponent submit will not score points. In some instances, chokes and armlocks can be applied in the standing position, although doing so is rare because greater movement is possible by the opponent when standing, making it easier for him or her to defend and escape.

Armlocks are executed by straightening the elbow joint, except for ude-garami (entangled armlock), which is performed with the elbow bent. Most chokes use the opponent's judogi (lapel) or involve the judoka's arm (for example, hadaka-jime, or naked choke). It is not permitted to choke with the fingers in an open hand around the throat.

Effective hold-downs involve holding the uke on his or her back and outside of his or her legs. If your opponent traps a leg or controls your torso in leg scissors, the hold is ineffective, even if the uke is on his or her back (for example, in guard position).

Ground techniques do not involve the preciseness of standing judo techniques. In standing judo, the fundamentals of moving, breaking balance, and throw entry require considerable practice. Timing is very important in standing judo and much of it is acquired through feel. These elements are not as emphasized in ground judo where many of the situations are isometric, and little movement and action seem to occur. In ground judo, contact with the opponent is closer, and the mat becomes an element in the action. Positional control in ground judo is important because many techniques must be executed from positions of advantage. It is therefore easier to see improvements in a shorter time period in ground judo than in standing. Many fighters will focus on ground judo if their aim is to improve as a fighter.

Tina Takahashi (age 11) controls her opponent in katame no waza.

An ineffective or broken hold. A hold is ineffective or broken when the tori is unable to get outside or free of the uke's legs in a scissor action. The judoka must be "outside" of the legs in order for a judo hold (osae-komi) to be effective.

Effective holding position is when the tori is able to control the opponent on the back and is positioned outside of the uke's legs. The tori should be prepared to move forward by making adjustments with the feet. The tori should also keep a tight grip on the uke's sleeve arm.

Ground judo is equally important to complement standing judo and is good training for overall judo development. The vast majority of champions are strong in both standing and ground judo. Some are especially noted for their strong ground fighting, such as Katsuhiko Kashiwazaki, Nobuyuki Sato, and Neil Adams. Even Yasuhiro Yamashita, although not regarded as a ground specialist, honed his ground skills and understood their importance. In fact, many of Yamashita's Olympic victories were won on the ground.

In ground judo there are some clear and distinct positions because contact between the fighters is much greater than in the standing position. Positions of neutrality do not occur as often as one would think. Conversely, in standing judo the majority of the time competitors are in positions of neutrality. In ground fighting, you or your opponent likely end up fighting from the guard, whether intentionally or not, or defending on "all fours," as in the turtle position. Fighting by turning away in the turtle position is not desired because it gives a position of advantage to the opponent.

When practicing ground judo, attempt quick, direct entries to better relate to the time frame you may encounter during competition. A more controlled, sequential approach is equally important to understand implications of position and for complete development of ground judo.

Phil Takahashi attempted kata-ha-jime on Eric Maurel at the '81 Worlds.

Turtle Position

The turtle position, or "all fours," is extremely defensive, and its only purpose is to block attacks and prevent the match from moving forward in ne-waza. It is a competition-only technique, and it is used to bring the match to a stalemate and force the referee to call, "Matte." In some cases, both fighters do not want to continue into ne-waza, and the match comes to a complete stop with both fighters waiting for the referee to call, "Matte" to restart the match in the standing position.

Tight turtle position for defense. Cross your arms, and keep your hands (thumbs) close to your neck and your elbows close to your knees. Close off space to prevent any attack. Once in the turtle position, be careful when moving out of it, for example, to attack or stand up, because this will expose your position to attack.

Tournament rules have actually encouraged use of the turtle position. Fighters know that by stalemating in the turtle position they will elude a disadvantaged ne-waza position and resume standing. Rules encourage standing action, and because ground judo takes time to develop and is perceived to be uninteresting by specatators, inactivity is stopped by the referee and the match resumed in the standing position. Judo matches have a time limit and a point-scoring system, which also has encouraged the use of purely defensive positions by the fighter who is leading in points. These positions can be used to burn off some clock time and allow a fighter several seconds to rest and regain composure.

In many cases the turtle position occurs after a blocked throw attempt. Some judoka immediately drop into this position to avoid being countered in the standing position or even use the position as a tactical move to avoid standing judo. In any case, the overall perception does not contribute to the spirit of attacking judo.

When ground fighting, you want to avoid going into turtle position. If you must go into turtle, close off space between your body, legs, and arms. Hold your neck and head down tight so that your chin closes off space for any choke attempt. You must stay "heavy" to keep stable so that you are not tipped or moved, thus allowing your opponent to hook under your body.

Flat Position

In the flat position, lay flat out on your stomach with your elbows tucked in tight to your body and your head down. The flat position is similar to the turtle position since you are conceding position except that you are lying flat to the mat. by going flat (prone) rather than staying up on your knees. Spread your legs out for stability or keep them together if your opponent is attempting leg rides. In the flat position, you must press down hard to the mat so your opponent cannot flip you over or get underneath your body. By taking a flat position, you are aiming for stalemate and are in a position of disadvantage.

The flat position enables you to press tightly against the tatami, allowing for a low and stable position. Stay close to the mat for greater stability and to close off space.

Keep close to the mat by anticipating attacks but be patient in waiting for the stalemate call by the official. The main techniques against these defensive positions are chokes and armlocks which are difficult and time consuming against a stubborn opponent. If however, you are on top, ahead on points, and want to run out the clock, then riding your opponent is a reasonably safe opportunity.

Guard Position

In guard position you are on your back with your opponent between your legs. This position is considered neutral because either partner is in position to attack. This is generally true, although because it is possible to attack from underneath, the degree of advantage will depend on the level of expertise of the opponent. A variation of the guard is inserting a foot or both feet inside to block the opponent's thigh (also called the butterfly guard). The butterfly guard position allows you to use your legs by blocking, pushing, and lifting. Use your legs by inserting your feet inside the uke's thighs.

Use your legs by inserting your feet inside the uke's thigh. You can push and control the uke in the butterfly positon with your knees pointing outward. Use your feet by pushing with your legs to keep the distance needed and to disrupt the uke's balance.

Guard Position-Attacking From Underneath

If you are in a defensive mode, attempt to prevent an attack from your opponent or to prevent your opponent from gaining position. Your aim is to achieve a stalemate position and return to standing by the referee's call of "Matte." If you are offensive, you are looking to attack from underneath (using a choke or armlock) or to roll the opponent and reverse position to apply a hold-down. The transition from defense to offense and vice-versa can occur quickly, and often the distinction between the two is not readily apparent. You can execute roll-over to go on the offensive.

You can execute techniques from underneath as in this choke (gyaku-juji-jime). Keep close to the uke and insert your hands deep when choking.

Tight roll over. You can execute roll over to go on the offensive.

Hand and arm action is like turning a steering wheel. Right foot lifts uke's leg up high to cause uke to land on his back.

Half-Guard Position

The half-guard position is similar to the guard position, but one leg of the top judoka has cleared the guard while the other leg is scissored or locked. In this position, the bottom judoka must ensure that the top judoka does not clear the second leg to acquire a "mount" position (osae-komi hold).

If you are on top, you are able to clear a leg and can progress to the half-guard position. Scoop your hiking arm under the uke's knee while your opposite free arm is kept short. Clear your leg over and across the uke's body. Use your hands to hold the uke from turning away toward your stomach.

Half-guard scissors to prevent osae-komi (hold down). A hold is ineffective if a half-guard or scissor position is initiated. Keep the scissor lock secure and tight above the uke's knee.

Holding Position

Aim for a stable position when holding or staying on top in the ground position. A wide base can be created using your arms and legs to increase stability. A flat or square body position that is low to the mat also helps to create stability and makes it more difficult for your opponent to roll or reverse the position. When holding it is important to control your upper body or head area so your opponent has more difficulty escaping.

Holding positons involve controlling your upper body and keeping a wide, low base. Your body is perpendicular to that of the uke's, with the legs apart to maximize stability. It is important to keep your chin down to prevent the uke from choking or being able to push your head with his free hand. Keep a wide, low base and adjust to the uke's movements when escaping.

Preventative Actions

Preventing the opponent from securing a hold in the first place is more desirable than attempting an escape once the hold is secured. Often, you can prevent hold-downs from occurring by using fundamental movements to block or prevent the opponent from gaining position.

Turning and Bridging

Turning and bridging movements are important for escaping from holds. It is important to drive your arm through when turning so your body follows and to prevent your opponent from trapping your arm to block the turn.

Bridging disrupts the hold by lifting and creating space so you can escape by turning. Use the uke's force and weight against herself by turning in and then turning away when she pushes back into you.

Ebi (Shrimp) Movements

By turning to either side and closing off the space between your elbow and leg, you can prevent the opponent from holding. The name "shrimp" (ebi) comes from the way shrimp swim, which is similar to the actions you use to flex your body to close off space to defend. The action "jackknifes" your body by pushing with your legs and bringing your hands to your feet.

Begin the ebi movement, a movement that is excellent for ground work, with your arms above your head.

Moving on the mat in a shrimplike action (ebi) allows you to retreat and close off space when being attacked. The action of reaching for your feet is used to move your body away. Alternate left and right actions. Push forward with your feet and reach for your toes with your hands to get full movement.

A different version of the shrimp movement focuses on keeping the elbow close to the body, which helps in escapes and moving out of holds before they become effective. In both positions it is important to always keep your head up and your legs bent (in front of the opponent). Bring your elbows down to your knees. Push forward with your feet, return to the start position, then repeat on the other side.

Control Grips
and Grip Breaks

Virtually every judoka has experienced the frustration of being subdued by superior gripping by a better opponent. Overly defensive postures, although discouraged and penalized, seem commonplace in today's competitive judo. The growth in the use of defensive posturing is an outcome of advancements in gripping technique and the resulting inevitable control of the opponent.

Gripping, or kumi-kata, can be considered an art in itself. In fact, gripping is so important for the judo fighter that rules were instituted on the length of the judogi sleeve and how tight it could be around the wrist. In boxing, the importance of having "fast" hands is often mentioned. In judo, too, fast hands are important, or rather the ability to fight for grip. Those unaccustomed to judo underestimate the quickness of the judoka's hands. It takes considerable training to acquire good gripping skills and to develop them to best suit your individual style. Gripping sequences are described in detail next.

GRIPPING SEQUENCES

Gripping is your first line of attack and defense. A great deal of time in a match is now devoted to securing your grip. Once you have the desired grip, you are able to control the match. This control makes gripping closely related to tactics. Figure 6.1 illustrates gripping sequence. At the start of the match the competitors stand apart.

When the referee calls "hajime" they begin the gripping sequence. They will engage and fight for grip by making contact with each other. Three basic positions are established as the competitors attempt to control each other: (1) advantage, (2) disadvantage, and (3) neutrality. A position of advantage or control allows you to attack. A position of disadvantage puts you on defense.

The judogi gives judoka the opportunity to control each other through effective methods of gripping. The tori can control the uke through gripping and thus dictate the action in the standing position. Getting the desired grip requires the tori to fight for a grip before the uke gets a grip.

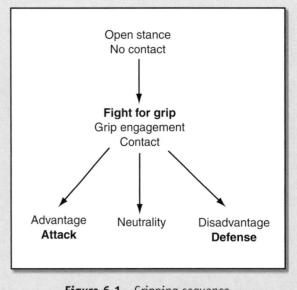

Figure 6.1 Gripping sequence.

Phil Takahashi's bronze medal victory at the 1981 Worlds is a good example of grip control. Phil managed to obtain his grip and attack with tai-otoshi in his match against Eric Maurel of France. Takahashi recalls: "Somehow I managed to get my grip. I was a little surprised I got it so easy, and I knew I had to attack fast." As it happened, Takahashi was able to control the grip and mount an offense. He scored waza-ari and several lower scores of koka and yuko. Finally, he ended the match with ippon and secured a bronze medal.

Key Points in Gripping

Once you have secured a grip, you can begin to execute certain techniques. The opponent will know this too. Therefore, it is preferable to secure a grip from which you can execute a number of techniques to keep your opponent from figuring out your next move. The basic sleeve-and-lapel grip is still a common and favorite grip because it allows the fighter to execute a variety of techniques.

Many fighters will attack quickly as soon as they have a grip, and some have developed the ability to attack with only one hand. You are well advised to prepare for fighting against these opponents by acquiring the ability to fight in the same way. Although gripping for offense is the main thrust, gripping for defense is also im-portant when you are trying to protect your lead or control the tempo of the match so you don't tire.

Judoka are incredibly strong in the hands because of the necessity to grip. It stands to reason then that you should develop strength in your hands and arms to improve gripping. Strengthening exercises include rope climbing, chinups, and wrist-curl exercises with a bar. To simulate the burning sensation in the forearms felt during a match (resulting from lactic-acid buildup), roll up a weight on a bar (called a "wrist-roller" exercise). Next, different grips are described.

Phil Takahashi attacks brother Ray in one of many matchups during their teen years. Phil grips Ray's judogi while Ray parries out of position with his body.

Basic Grip

Grip your lapel hand (tsurite) near your opponent's upper chest and your sleeve hand (hikite) below his or her elbow. Grip tight and relax your arms. Place the grip tension mainly in your little fingers rather than in your entire hand to maintain flexibility in your wrists.

Most judo techniques can be performed with a basic grip. Some techniques, such as sumi-gaeshi and uki-waza, require changes to the basic grip such as those demonstrated in nage no kata. Some grip adjustments are made in the throws that represent armored warriors fighting on the battlefield in feudal times.

Pulling-Action-of-the-Sleeve Grip: Hikite

In kuzushi of the sleeve grip in many forward throws, you must both lift and disrupt the balance of the uke in a forward direction. The action of your pulling arm should resemble the pull you would use when starting a lawn mower. Turn your hand so that it faces outward to maximize the length of the pull. It also provides the lift needed to raise your opponent's center of gravity, making it easier to execute a throw.

Basic grip. Starting from a natural grip, grip your opponent's lapel with your right hand and his right sleeve under the elbow with your left hand.

Hikite pull. The pulling action on the hikite grip breaks the uke's balance forward. Pull your arm so the palm of your hand faces down and your elbow points up and out at shoulder level for a long pull.

Lapel Grip: Tsurite

The lapel grip, or tsurite, is also called the "playing" hand. The Japanese word "tsuri" means "to fish," which mimics the flicking action of the wrist required in this grip. Much of the work of the grip lifts, although the tsurite also generates good pulling and pushing actions because of the tightness of the grip and lapel to the opponent's body. In a basic lapel grip, your hand grips at the opponent's chest. A low grip, closer to the opponent's stomach, is not often used because it is more difficult to generate kuzushi, or off balancing, from this position. A higher lapel grip is used more often, and numerous throws can be executed with the hand located near or around the collar.

Tsurite pull. The gripping hand can pull, push, lift, and block. Work the tsurite grip in conjunction with the hikite grip to maximize breaking of your opponent's balance.

Little Finger Tight

Ray Takahashi recalls: "My father always said to us, 'Grip with your little finger tight.' At the time, when we were kids, it didn't make sense to us." Gripping with the little finger tight allows for a secure and flexible wrist because when the little finger squeezes tight it allows the thumb to stay loose and flexible. Having a supple and flexible wrist allows you to move your arms quickly and to relax your arms when needed so they are not overly stiff. This flexibility saves energy and keeps you from tiring over the course of the match. Gripping with the little finger tight is the correct way to execute any grip.

Squeeze the grip tightly by using the little fingers, but try not to be stiff at the wrist.

Variations to the basic lapel grip allow for some techniques to be executed easier and prevent the opponent from erecting a good defense. Major types of lapel grips include the following:

High Lapel Grip

Grip high but not around the collar. Make quick adjustments with your hand so that you can switch from controlling your opponent's head to a lower basic grip position. The high lapel grip and the behind-the-neck grip are often used by uchi-mata specialists. They are often used by taller opponents. A shorter person using these grips would be stretched out and therefore vulnerable.

Double-Lapel Grip

Place both hands on the upper lapels. The double-lapel grip is good for both left and right attacks. The disadvantage of the double-lapel grip is that your opponent's arms are completely free.

Armpit, Belt Grip

The armpit grip allows you to execute a strong pull because the pull is "shorter" than the sleeve grip and pulls the body rather than the arm. By straightening or pushing the arm, distance from the opponent can be maintained if necessary. Gripping your opponent's belt tightly also allows you to generate good pull and contact. This is good for strong control of your opponent's body. The disadvantage of this grip is that your opponent has both arms free, and may be able to prevent a clean throw by hanging on to you or by putting his or her hands down on the mat. Since you must attack within five seconds of gripping the belt, your opponent knows that you will attack or release the grip and will be prepared.

High lapel grip.

Double-lapel grip.

Armpit, belt grip.

Behind-the-Neck Grip

Insert your thumb behind the uke's neck to control his or her upper body and head. When performing a forward throw, disrupt the uke's balance by moving his or her head with a strong forward pull. This grip is useful against shorter opponents or opponents who use a hunched fighting position. It is very effective in controlling your opponent's body since it is very easy to move his or her head with a jerk. This will momentarily disrupt his orientation. This grip can result in pulling the gi over your opponent's head, resulting in the referee calling matte.

Back-of-Gi Grip

Grip the back of the uke's judogi by reaching over the uke's shoulder to generate a strong pull. Gripping behind the back is ideal for major front throws, although you can use a downward and sideways pull to keep the uke from anticipating what attack you will be taking. The opportunity for the back-of-gi grip may arise when the opponent has stumbled or gone down to block a throw. When he or she comes up, there will be an instant when uchi-mata using this grip are possible. Keep tension on the gi between the opponent's armpits (across his or her back) with your fingers under a fold.

Low-Sleeve Grip

Grip between the uke's elbow and the end of his or her sleeve. The low-sleeve grip is not only good for pushing to keep the uke away but also for executing attacks. The low-sleeve grip is effective in neutralizing your opponent's grip on your lapel. With a jerk downward, you may be able to break his or her grip, giving you momentarily complete control over his or her grip.

Behind-the-neck grip.

Back-of-gi grip.

Low-sleeve grip.

High-Sleeve Grip

Grip above the elbow behind the uke's tricep. The high-sleeve grip provides diversity in attack because of the deep pulling action it can create. When pulling, turn so your palm faces down. The high-sleeve grip is easy to maintain since the gi is loose and your opponent does not have an effective method to break it. Your control over your opponent's arm is limited, however.

Under-Elbow Grip

The grip is directly under the uke's elbow. By turning your hand to point your thumb toward the uke's body, the under-elbow grip can be used to push the uke's elbow up for sode-tsurikomi-goshi. The under-elbow grip is useful in controlling your opponent's arm, and can be used offensively and defensively. Your opponent can break your grip by bending his or her elbow (stretching the gi) and pulling.

Cross Grip

Reach across to grip on the same side as the sleeve arm. Usually, the cross grip indicates an attack will follow to the side of the grip so the attack must be executed quickly. The cross grip can be used only momentarily when surprising your opponent, or when taking advantage of his or her loss of balance from a setup move or attack.

High-sleeve grip.

Under-elbow grip.

Cross grip.

End-of-Sleeve Grip

Grip at the end of the sleeve to control the uke's arm. The end-of-sleeve grip is good for preventing the uke from getting a grip and then quickly attacking with a long pull. Immediately take the opportunity to get the end-of-sleeve grip. You will have complete control of your opponent's arm until he or she breaks free of your grip or gets hold of your lapel.

Double-Sleeve Grip

The double-sleeve grip allows you to choose a right- or left-side attack. Controlling the sleeves prevents the uke from getting a grip. Tori grips the end of uke's sleeves before uke can take a grip. The "little" fingers should scoop the sleeve from the outside so as to turn the sleeve inside out to secure a tight grip. Make sure that you do not insert your fingers inside the uke's sleeve. Inserting your fingers inside the sleeve is a penalty, since it is dangerous to get your fingers trapped in the sleeve.

Belt Grip

With the belt grip, it is necessary to attack your opponent immediately. Grip over the top to osoto-gari, harai-goshi. The deep, over-the-back belt grip allows you to pull the uke in tight. Be aware that by opening up your side as you make the belt grip, you become vulnerable to a lift (for example, te-guruma). The belt grip can be used when uke is much shorter or bends low exposing one's backside and belt. Tori can reach over uke and take the belt grip with uke's head positioned to the outside of the arm on the belt.

End-of-sleeve grip.

Double-sleeve grip.

Belt grip.

Left-Side Grip

When the uke has a right-sided grip, the tori can initiate a left-sided grip. Using opposite left or right grips is kenka-yotsu. A left-handed grip may be unusual for your opponent, and his or her lack of experience will be an advantage for you.

Left-side grip.

Stand-Up Grip

Stand up straight and exert force downward on the uke. Downward pressure makes it difficult for the uke to attack. You can watch and feel your opponent quite well in this position.

Stand-up grip.

Exaggerated Right Stance

Exaggerate a right grip by pulling your left arm back while pushing with your right arm. Place your right leg forward. Your left hand should pull down on the uke's arm, much like pulling back your arm to prepare to shoot an arrow from a bow. Control your opponent by moving his body and studying his reactions.

Exaggerated right stance.

Stiff Arms

Keep the uke back by extending or stiffening your arms straight to prevent an attack. Keep your arms close to your body while pushing. Squeeze your little finger and move your hands toward your thumb. Your muscles should be flexed so your opponent cannot move around.

Stiff arms.

Crunching Arms

Once you have acquired a secure, comfortable grip, contract heavily to close off any movement or attacking opportunity. The grip makes the uke look defensive and can be used tactically when appropriate. Be on guard when applying crunching arms as the uke will likely attempt to move quickly to get out of a defensive position, especially once you release the grip of crunching arms. Be prepared to attack when you release some control over the uke.

Crunching arms.

GRIP BREAKS

Now that we have learned common grips, the obvious next step is to learn common grip breaks. Common grip breaks include the following:

Catch Hands

As the uke reaches, catch his or hands by meeting them head on with your hands up. Intertwining fingers and bending and twisting are prohibited. Know the limitations when engaging in this grip break.

a

After "Hajime" the fight for grip begins.

b

Catching your opponent's hands allows some momentary control.

Deflect Hands

When the uke reaches with the right hand, deflect it inward by slapping it quickly with your left hand. Ensure that the block precedes the deflection of your right hand. Note how the left hand is raised and used to block if necessary.

Deflection from the outside.

Deflection from the inside.

Ready for deflection and getting a grip.

Blocks

As the uke reaches with the right hand, block with your left hand by moving the uke's hand up and outward. Keep the hands up when vying for a grip from the out-side. Block and take a grip using your left arm at the uke's right wrist or sleeve if the opportunity exists. As you block the uke's initial reach, be cautious of the uke's left hand by meeting it with your right hand.

It is easier to prevent your opponent from getting a grip on your lapel if you block from the inside.

Be prepared to block your opponent's other hand.

Hold Your Lapel

With this grip break, the uke has a left-handed grip on your lapel. You reach inside with your right arm to grip the uke's left lapel. Grip your own lapel while simultane-ously gripping and pulling your own lapel away with your right hand. Move your body away while turning to the left and pulling with a hard jerking action to break the grip. Initiate the grip break before the uke has a strong, tight grip.

Your opponent has managed to get ahold of your right lapel from above.

Reach under to get your opponent's lapel. Push away to stretch out his arm. At the same time, pull your lapel out of his grip.

Bend to Tighten at Elbow

When the uke grips or attempts to grip your sleeve with his or her left hand, bend your elbow to tighten your judogi, making it difficult to grip. For maximum effectiveness, it's best to initiate the elbow bend just before a secure grip can be acquired. As you bend the elbow, use your left arm to slap or push the gripping arm away. Use forceful, quick actions and move your body back while pulling your arm away.

Uke has a grip under the tori's elbow.

Bending your elbow will stretch out the cloth of your sleeve, making it harder for the uke to keep a grip. It may be necessary to use your left hand to help break the grip.

Single-Arm Push-Down

The strong grip is very important and can really dominate and nullify your opponent's movement. Strong arms and hands are important in gripping.

If the uke's grip with the right hand does not break on the tori's left lapel, it is possible for the tori to control the grip by extending the arm and pushing the uke's right arm away. If the uke pulls back with his arm, the tori should use the action to attack in the direction of the pull.

Reverse angle view. The tori grips low on the uke's right sleeve with the left hand and pushes down to prevent the uke from gripping. The tori extends the arm down and away. Tori initiates the grip break before the uke has a strong and secure grip.

Two-Handed Lapel-Break Push

Use both hands to grip the uke's sleeve and push away forcefully to break the grip. Grip your hands close together to prevent the uke's sleeve from slipping on his or her own arm. Pushing the uke's arm sideways prevents this slipping.

Grips on the lapel are often very hard to break because of the looseness of the gi. With this technique, you may be able to break the uke's grip on your lapel and keep the grip on his or her sleeve.

The tori grips the uke's sleeve with the left (outside) hand, and uses the right hand to grip the uke's right hand.

The tori pushes down and away with the hands while moving the body back to break the grip. The tori pushes the right hand outward and away against the uke's gripped hand. The outward push loosens the grip, and pushing away breaks the grip on the tori's lapel.

Sleeve-Grip Break With Leg

With this technique, you use a leg to help break the grip. It would be best to follow through with an attack immediately. Don't use this break too often since your opponent may be able to take advantage of your reaction to his or her grip.

The tori reaches back with the right hand that is gripped by the uke's left hand. The tori grips behind her right knee.

The tori moves the right leg back to break the uke's grip while keeping the uke away by pushing with the left arm.

Sleeve-Grip Break–Cut

This is a common technique for getting your arm free. Before doing it, make sure that you already have a follow-up plan of attack.

The tori lifts the gripped right arm and points the elbow outward. The tori initiates this action quickly because it opens up her side for an instant.

The tori pulls back quickly and forcefully to cut and break the grip by turning the body to the right. The tori should be prepared to use the left arm to keep the uke away in case he attacks.

GRASPING

Grasping can be differentiated from gripping because in grasping you often grab the opponent's body part, such as the leg in morote-gari, rather than the judogi pant leg that gripping entails. Some competition techniques have evolved where grasping has become prevalent to make the technique work. In morote-gari, you can quickly grasp the opponent behind the knees with your hands and drive forward with your body to make the throw work. The advantages of grasping are being able to quickly secure or block, versus gripping which requires one to obtain the grip first before a block, pull, or push can be performed. Grasping also allows you to get closer to the opponent—even a few inches closer can make a difference in morote-gari, which is now executed in a style similar to that of a double-leg takedown in wrestling. Judoka now often grasp behind the leg like in a wrestling attack rather than grip the judogi pant leg as has been traditionally taught in judo.

Kata-guruma is a popular competition technique derived from wrestling. In kata-guruma, the tori takes a high grip behind the uke's arm, almost like a grasp, so a strong pull can be made to off balance the uke forward.

Both grasping *(a)* and gripping *(b)* can be used in judo and are used interchangeably when executing kata-guruma—fireman's carry style. Note how the hand is open to capture the arm. The open hand allows the tori to hook the arm and pull tightly down for attacks such as kata-guruma. When grasping, the tori aims to reach as high as possible and make a hooking action with the hand. Note how the hand grasps the upper arm of the uke compared to the more traditional grip on the judogi.

OVEREMPHASIZING GRIP FIGHTING

Overemphasizing grip fighting has become an unfortunate attitude prevalent in competition where the fight for grip has resulted in the development of overly defensive tactics that go against the spirit of judo. In fact, to prevent the opponent from getting a good grip, European judogis were made thicker in the early 1990s. It was found lapels were up to two times thicker than the average Japanese lapel. A previous rule for sleeve length and size had been implemented for similar reasons.

Overemphasizing gripping in randori can hinder your overall judo development because it will prevent you from engaging in a multitude of situations and dynamic actions. This can happen if you spend too much time grip fighting, escaping and defending from a grip, or obtaining a particular grip. British judo star, Neil Adams, puts it this way: "For judo to continue to evolve in a positive way, we have to ensure that the traditional, fast, dynamic techniques are complemented, not ruined, by developments, in kumi-kata (gripping)" (*Grips*. N. Adams. 1990. The Crowood Press. Wiltshire. Pg. 11). Make a conscious effort to use a variety of grips as well as to allow your partner to do the same during training. Try to be open in randori to experiencing all types of situations from both an offensive and defensive perspective.

Standing Combinations and Counters

In judo, the ability to use combination techniques forms the basis of technical and tactical applications. Combination techniques can be defined as the application of several techniques in rapid succession, moving from one to the next in a smooth unbroken sequence (*Kodokan New Japanese-English Dictionary of Judo.* Teizo Kawamura and Toshiro Daigo. 2000. Kodokan Judo Institute. Tokyo. Pg. 110). The speed of attack of an executed technique is critical for its success. An attack must be executed so fast that the opponent has no time to react. In competitive judo, however, fighters are trained for both attack and defense so that one cannot rely on pure speed for technical success.

Combination techniques refer to two or more techniques that are linked together. In fact, most judoka use combination techniques in their judo whether they know it or not. In the sport of boxing, combination punches are commonly understood, such as when the boxer sets up his punch with a series of jabs. Similarly, in judo, the importance of combining techniques is quickly realized by tournament fighters who have felt the frustration of being unable to execute the various techniques they learned in the dojo against a resisting opponent.

In competition, the action is fast and dynamic. You must be able to assess the situation, choose a particular technique, and execute it before the opponent can react or defend against the technique you have chosen. The level of sophistication of technique has increased with modern judo where variations are now too numerous to be classified in the gokyo, which represented the standard series of throwing techniques. As you become more proficient in your technical development, variations to techniques

Although Phil Takahashi throws his opponent, the throwing action has changed in the dynamism of competition so that it does not resemble a technique performed with a cooperative uke. This situation illustrates that preciseness is needed to execute techniques successfully.

will emerge, many of which you can modify to suit your individual style, body type, and physical and technical capabilities.

Most advanced fighters have a good technical background and are able to perform techniques well in the dojo. The challenge then is to bridge the gap from static demonstration of technique to a dynamic, resistive setting in randori and in competition. Attacks with a singular technique, if not executed precisely, are easier for the opponent to counter. Combination attacks make countering by the opponent more difficult and therefore are often more successful.

COMBINATION TECHNIQUES AT WORK

Combination techniques have slight differences in application, and it is important to understand how they work so you can apply them as effectively as possible. Combination techniques can be broken down into three major types: (1) action–reaction, such as fakes (e.g., thrower fakes going in one direction in order to fool opponent to get a reaction); (2) ballistic sequences that are used as setups (e.g., when the thrower uses an entry technique in order to follow-up with the main technique); and (3) moving from one technique to another (e.g, when the first technique is blocked or diverted and the thrower moves directly into another). Action–reaction combinations are based upon the opponent's reaction to an initial attack. Ballistic combinations link techniques together in rapid succession so they are like one attack. Last, moving from one technique to another requires a quick assessment of the opponent's reaction with a follow-up attack to link techniques in a sequence. In a ballistic combination you don't wait for, but anticipate the opponent's reaction. It's a little riskier, but may be more successful because it's faster. Moving from one technique to another is not predetermined but requires a quick evaluation by the judoka to continue different attacks when the opponent is in positions of disadvantage. For example, the judoka may attack with a throw and move quickly into osae-waza (holding techniques) while the opponent is attempting to recover.

The ouchi-gari–tai-otoshi combination is discussed next. This combination can be performed using either the action–reaction combination or the ballistic combination. Although both have the same result, that is, to throw the opponent, they work as a result of different concepts.

Action–Reaction Combination: Ouchi-Gari–Tai-Otoshi

In the action–reaction combination, the judoka attacks the opponent backward with ouchi-gari (the fake) and waits for the opponent to react by stepping out of the attack and pushing forward. The judoka re-attacks with tai-otoshi, completing the combination (ouchi-gari → tai- otoshi). It is important to note that the actions were all predetermined. That is, the judoka always had the intention to end the attack with tai-otoshi.

The important principle in this case is the reaction of the opponent to the fake (ouchi-gari) and how the judoka utilizes the opponent's reaction to follow up with another attack—hence, the combination attack. Action–reaction combinations work well because there is a natural reaction from the opponent, whether intentional or not, to an action or attack. From a biomechanical point of view, this principle is based upon the third law of motion that states that for every action there is an equal and opposite reaction.

Although action–reaction combinations are likely the most commonly used combination techniques, other concepts are applied as well.

The tori attacks with ouchi-gari and pushes the uke backward.

The reaction of the uke is to push back while stepping out of the throw. The tori plants the left leg on the mat when the uke steps out of the attack.

As the uke reacts by pushing forward, the tori turns to attack and moves the back leg (right) close to the uke's stance to position the body for tai-otoshi.

The tori executes tai-otoshi by stepping across with the left leg, utilizing the uke's reaction to ouchi-gari.

Ballistic Combination: Ouchi-Gari → Tai-Otoshi

A ballistic combination attack is executed fast so the intended attack (tai-otoshi) is executed immediately after the delivery of the fake (ouchi-gari). In this case, the judoka assumes the opponent falls for the fake and starts executing the tai-otoshi before finding out whether the opponent did or not. The ouchi-gari is meant to load the support leg of the opponent and put him or her in a position of vulnerability. The judoka, knowing this, must make a quick attack with tai-otoshi to complete the combination.

The ballistic combination is as close as one can get in putting two techniques together to become a single sequential attack. The difference between the ballistic and the action–reaction combination is based upon the time lapse between the fake and the intended attack. A longer time would allow you to assess the reaction of the opponent (for example, opponent pushes back from the ouchi-gari fake). In the ballistic combination, the time frame between the preplanned fake and intended attack is too short, so you do not have the time to assess the reaction of the opponent. You just assume that the fake will work and go ahead and sequence the attack.

The danger of using a ballistic combination is that if you don't effectively set up the opponent with the initial fake, you can be countered while applying the combination. This almost happened to Phil Takahashi when his back foot slipped when executing the tai-otoshi. He recalls using a ballistic combination (ouchi-gari → tai-otoshi) to win the bronze medal at the 1981 World Championships in Maastricht: "Once I got my left grip I knew I had to attack quickly. You don't get many chances to use one of your best techniques in a match. I stepped in hard and hopped into the throw. I slipped slightly on my support leg, but I was able to finish and score waza-ari."

The tori attacks with an ouchi-gari fake with the left foot by planting it inside the uke's right foot to transfer the uke's weight to his left foot. The tori attacks on an angle rather than straight on.	The tori hops to move the right foot (back leg) closer while reaching with the left foot across the uke's body for tai-otoshi. The tori must pull with the right hand to break the uke's balance and keep weight over the left foot. It is important to put weight on the uke's left leg that now supports his weight.	The tori attacks quickly with tai-otoshi while the uke is off balance and then follows through by springing with the legs and pulling with the right arm.

Another weakness of the ballistic combination, although not as severe in consequence, happens if you move too quickly and the opponent does not respond to the initial fake but does respond to the intended attack. The result is an unsuccessful combination attack.

In order for you to best utilize combination techniques based upon these concepts, movement must occur, that is, you must be able to move the opponent. This ability to move the opponent is called kuzushi and tai-sabaki (see chapter 6) and involves the ability to break the opponent's balance and move and change directions while reacting to the opponent. Kuzushi and tai-sabaki, however, should not be confused with moving from one technique to another, the last major type of combination technique.

Moving From One Technique to Another

The ability to move from one technique to another was one of Yasuhiro Yamashita's fortes. His ability to attack and then re-attack quickly enabled him to catch the opponent off-guard before he had time to recover or know what Yamashita was doing. The concept of moving from one technique to another is very similar to the previous two combinations, but the difference lies in the follow-up technique, which is not predetermined. The transition from standing to ground judo is a good example of how one moves from one technique to another. Moving from one technique to another requires the ability to attack in a controlled, relentless manner so the opponent has no ability to recover. The ability to recognize a position of vulnerability and to select the appropriate technique in response and apply it quickly is key. This combination technique requires an offensive mind-set.

Masao Takahashi controls his opponent after throwing him with okuri-ashi-barai by making a smooth transition from standing to ground judo. Note the wide base created by Takahashi's legs and the square position to the mat for greater stability.

Practicing combination attacks requires good cooperation with one's uke because the situational objective requires certain reactions that make it work. On the one hand, too much resistance hinders timing and the ability to create the specific action to be practiced. On the other hand, too little resistance does not provide realistic reactions to replicate what may happen in a more resistive situation. It is important that both the uke and the tori understand the objective of what is to be practiced. In other words, practicing the combination ouchi-gari → tai-otoshi seems easy enough. But, many beginners, and even more experienced fighters, end up practicing something else. For example, if the uke reacts too early by pushing forward immediately and does not step back from the ouchi-gari attack the tori is forced to react differently. In this situation the action–reaction combination is not practiced.

Practicing combinations requires cooperation because the uke must provide the correct reaction for combinations to work. If the reaction is incorrect, such as when the uke does not provide a realistic reaction to the ouchi-gari, the combination cannot be performed. This makes it difficult to practice the combination as it would occur in a real match situation. In *b* the uke does not react from the ouchi-gari attack by pushing forward. This makes the follow-up attack of tai-otoshi by the tori not only difficult, but would be a wrong choice for a combination attack.

Osoto-Gari (Left) Feint → Ippon-Seoi-Nage (Right)

This is a good combination attack feinting left osoto-gari (major outer reaping throw), creating a reaction from the uke so the tori finds an opening for a seoi-nage (right shoulder throw).

The tori makes a preliminary fake attack with osoto-gari to induce a reaction. The tori makes sure the left hand has the desired grip before the osoto-gari attack— either a high-sleeve or lapel grip— for ippon-seoi-nage.

As the tori retreats back from the osoto-gari, the uke swings the body around quickly by circling the retreating left leg around while pivoting on the right foot. The key is for the tori to swing back the attack leg quickly from osoto-gari and pivot with speed into seoi-nage.

The tori bends and fits the body into position for ippon-seoi-nage ready to finish the throw.

Ouchi-Gari → Kata-Guruma

The ouchi-gari is more of a step-in than a really strong reap. The pulling hand is very important in this movement, and the chin and back must be kept in alignment. The movement consists of driving up and towards the uke as you lift. The shoulders and the head drive in as you move in toward the uke. The pulling is kept strong throughout the movement to prevent countering by the uke.

Phil Takahashi lifts his opponent with kata-guruma at the 1981 World Championships.

a

The tori attacks with right ouchi-gari.

b

As the uke steps out of the ouchi-gari, the tori enters with kata-guruma.

c

The tori attacks from the knees to keep a stable base. The tori places his right hand behind the uke's right knee.

d

The tori pulls down with the left arm while lifting with the right arm.

e

Sitting version: The tori penetrates by sitting on the right leg. This version can be performed in place of entering on both knees.

f

The tori follows through with the kata-guruma attack by springing in the ankles and hips and simultaneously pulling down with the left arm and lifting with the right arm.

Osoto-Gari → Hiza-Guruma

This technique was a favorite of Olympic coach, Hiroshi Nakamura of Canada, who was known for his devastating osoto-gari in Japan. His powerful and big step along with a swinging action of his upper body to complete the throw resembled a kind of centrifugal force of an Olympic hammer thrower.

The attacking leg of osoto-gari is a slight feint only to make the uke resist and react forward. Tori uses the momentum to apply the hiza-guruma (knee wheel). The tori must pull hard with the collar grip to make the hiza-guruma work.

The tori enters osoto-gari by stepping with the right leg to the side and attacking with the left leg. The tori retreats out and does not follow through with the attack.

The tori enters again, faking the osoto-gari, stepping with the right leg to the side. As the uke reacts to the osoto-gari attack, the tori switches to hiza-guruma.

The tori blocks the uke's right knee and pulls hard with the left hand while pivoting on the right foot to turn the body toward the uke. The tori follows through with hiza-guruma and throws the uke over. The tori holds the left foot that blocks the uke's knee as long as possible into the throw.

Ippon-Seoi-Nage → Kouchi-Makikomi

This technique was a favorite technique and one of Ray Takahashi's first to give him success in his years as a junior. It was taught to Ray by his mother, June, in the mid-'60s. The ippon-seoi-nage is used to get uke to react so that he or she is unbalanced to the rear. Tori applies a deep kouchi-gari and grasps uke's leg to prevent his or her escape.

Ray Takahashi executing a kouchi-makikomi during his early teens.

a

The tori fakes with ippon-seoi-nage by moving the right leg into the uke's stance while entering the right arm under the uke's right arm.

b

As the uke reacts backward to the front fake (ippon-seoi-nage), the tori lowers own body pulling the left hand down.

c

The tori scoops with the right leg to the uke's right leg and reaches down with the right hand to the uke's leg. The tori drives the uke back by lowering his body and keeping contact. If the tori wraps the right leg around the uke's right leg the throw becomes kouchi-makikomi, considered a sacrifice because the tori's body is positioned such that the tori falls toward his back.

Kouchi-Gari → Yoko-Tomoe-Nage

Tomoe-nage was made popular by Olympic and world champion, Takao Kawaguchi in the early '70s and Yasuhiko Moriwaki and Katsuhiko Kashiwazaki in the '80s. Luis Shinohara of Brazil defeated Phil Takahashi at the '84 Olympics by a split decision on the technique although it didn't score.

Tori uses the kouchi-gari to unbalance uke to the rear. Uke's reaction by stepping back and then leaning forward gives tori the opportunity to apply the yoko-tomoe-nage. The sideways version is done very quickly.

Phil Takahashi scores ippon with yoko-tomoe-nage.

a

The tori attacks with kouchi-gari with the right leg, making the uke step back thus creating space.

b

The uke reacts forward from the kouchi-gari fake. The tori plants the right leg after the kouchi-gari attack and lifts the left leg to initiate tomoe-nage by falling toward his back. The tori places the kicking leg low on the uke's stomach and keeps it bent until the tori is on his back.

c

The tori falls back sideways, pointing his head toward the uke's right side. The tori kicks the uke over for the throw, pulling down on the left arm while pushing with the right.

Kouchi-Gari → Kuchiki-Taoshi

Kuchiki-taoshi and other leg-grabbing techniques are extensively used in competitions. When uke reacts by lifting his or her leg to avoid being thrown by kouchi-gari, tori catches the leg and drives uke backward with kuchiki-taoshi.

Phil Takahashi does a kouchi-gari → kuchiki-taoshi on Art Hamade of British Columbia in 1974.

Tori attacks with kouchi-gari using the right foot.

The tori expects the uke to react by lifting the attacked leg out of the kouchi-gari. Before the uke can step out of the kouchi-gari attack, the tori uses the left hand to reach behind the uke's attacked leg. The tori plants the right leg on the mat to keep balance while driving forward.

The tori angles the attack to the left so the uke's weight transfers to the attack leg (left), which is taken out. The tori drives forward with the right arm, pushing the uke back.

119

Uchi-Mata Fake → Tani-Otoshi

A strong pull, a jump behind, and close contact are required to ensure this combination is effective. Be wary of leaving space as the thrower can counter your combination with uchi-mata if your attack is loose. Be careful not to fall sideways on the uke's knees.

The tori turns the body slightly forward and lifts the right leg to fake an uchi-mata attack. The tori must keep the left leg outside of the uke's stance and the body positioned in line with the uke sideways.

When the uke reacts to the uchi-mata by pulling backward, the tori retreats, checks the right leg, and slides it behind uke's body.

The tori traps the uke with the extended leg and pulls hard with the right hand to execute tani-otoshi.

Kouchi-Gari → Uchi-Mata

Uchi-mata is the most popular tournament technique. The following photos illustrate a common setup or combination for uchi-mata. The kouchi-gari is more of a step than a real reap.

Tori attacks with kouchi-gari.

Uke reacts by retreating right foot. Tori plants right foot in front of uke's right foot.

The tori quickly moves the left leg back as close to the middle of the uke's feet as possible. The tori's left leg (back leg) steps behind the right and is kept bent so that when the throw is initiated the lift can be generated.

The tori continues into uchi-mata, pulling hard with the left hand, and lifts uke by sweeping his right leg onto uke's inner-left thigh.

Kouchi–Gari → Kata-Guruma

The kouchi-gari allows an initial distraction and a good deep step towards the uke. The tori's head is kept up high under the uke's armpit. A strong pull with the left arm prevents the uke from countering. The tori drives the uke forward and up simultaneously.

The tori attacks with kouchi-gari to get the uke to step back, creating space for attack. It is important for the tori to keep a tight grip to ensure the balance of the uke can be disrupted.

The tori pulls the uke while attacking forward and reaching for the inside of the uke's right leg. The tori attacks with a deep step by trying to get his shoulder under the uke's body.

The tori throws the uke over his shoulders by pulling with his left arm and raising his body and lifting with his right arm. The tori pulls the arm down rather than up and across. This allows for good contact when attacking.

Kosoto-Gake (Right) → Okuri-Ashi-Barai (Left)

When both you and your opponent are locked into strong grips, your footwork can make the all-important difference. From an extreme stance pulling hard on the opponent's collar and sleeve, clip his or her far leg, and then follow up with a sweep.

| The tori pushes the uke backward as he attacks with his right leg with kosoto-gake. | The tori continues to push so the uke must step out and put weight on the foot after stepping out. | As the uke moves backward from stepping out, the tori sweeps with the opposite leg when the uke's weight is taken off the right foot. |

Deashi-Barai → Sode-Tsurikomi-Goshi

The tori exaggerates a deashi fake but misses the uke's leg and swings it across to step into sode-tsurikomi-goshi.

The tori attacks with deashi-barai. The tori grips with the right hand under the uke's elbow.

The tori sweeps the leg, mimicking the deashi attack but instead sweeping across the uke's body. The uke reacts by believing it is an attack by deashi-barai. The tori overemphasizes the deashi attack so the uke believes the attack is real.

The tori continues the action and steps across the uke and enters into sode-tsurikomi-goshi. The tori pushes up on the uke's elbow as he sweeps across the uke's body.

The tori finishes the sode-tsurikomi-goshi throw.

COUNTERS: KAESHI WAZA

Counters are often overlooked in the teaching of judo. This oversight may be because, in the past, counters were associated with fighters who resort to wrestling or sambo applications. The use of power and many of its unorthodox movements have distanced counters from classical judo teachings. Nonetheless, it is important to recognize counters quickly and apply technique to an existing attack.

The classical counters of utsuri-goshi and ura-nage (kata style) are precise in timing and require great skill. Yet, some still hold the notion that counters are associated with "unpolished" judo. Certainly, counterattacks and their style are more prevalent in Russia and Eastern Europe, which does little to alleviate this view. Classical counters are applied infrequently in contest judo, giving way to other counter techniques such as tani-otoshi applications and pick-up variations (sukui-nage), which are also used as direct attacking techniques. Yet, counters do involve complex movements and athleticism, such as "drawing" the opponent in to attack by leaving an opening. Robert Van de Walle, Olympic champion (1980) and well-known for his counters comments on his use of pick-ups: "I had to use technique and timing. . . I learned to execute them with finesse." (Robert Van de Walle. *Pick-ups*, 1993. Ippon Books Ltd. London. Pg. 7).

One method of classifying defense is to describe the progression through three lines of defense, depending on the extent of the attack and when defense is initiated (see table 7.1). Using arms and body movement make the first line of defense. In this line, the judoka is able to prevent the opponent from attacking at all by gripping and moving out of position. The first line of defense is preferred because it prevents the opponent from making an attack. Unfortunately, overemphasis of this line can look too defensive and, at worst, can lead to poor posture and an attitude that may contribute to inactivity and negative judo.

The second line of defense is characterized by defending when the opponent has executed an attack but is unable to finish. The judoka is able to defend by reacting, resisting, and moving out from the attack. The distinguishing factor in the second line of defense is that the judoka aims to defend to achieve neutrality, that is, to defend against the attack and not be thrown.

The last or third line of defense is counterattacking. In this case, the judoka attacks the opponent's attack (counter) for one of two reasons: Either the judoka believes a counter is possible (a poor attack by the opponent), or a counterattack

Phil Takahashi counters brother Allyn with utsuri-goshi (left-changing hip, or hip-shift throw) at the 1972 CNE International in Toronto, Canada.

Table 7.1—Three Lines of Defense				
Line	Description	Attack progression (osoto-gari)	Defensive description	Position of advantage or disadvantage
First line of defense	Gripping, evasion, tai-sabaki	Osoto-gari attempt; kuzushi and preliminary movement with attacking leg	Block attack with arms; move back out of attacking position	Attacker has not gained advantage with attack. Defense is in favorable position to defend attack.
Second line of defense	Resisting out of the attack	Attacker makes leg contact and initiates actions to throw	Resistance and defender lifts attacked leg up and out	Both attacker and defender are in uncertain positions. Neither has a distinct advantage over the other.
Third line of defense	Countering, twisting out of the throw	Attacker continues into the throw	Transfer weight to attacked leg; counter with own osoto-gari	Attacker has a distinct advantage because the progression of the attack has progressed past position of neutrality.

Note: The third line of defense can be intentional. That is, a very skilled judoka can not only "wait" to apply a third-line defense but can also make it look easy. The judoka "allows" an osoto-gari attack to progress to a point where an intentional counter can be made.

is the only way out without being thrown. To clarify, let's say the judoka has been attacked by ouchi-gari. If the judoka reads the attack as it's being executed, she can prepare to counter with ashi-waza. But, if the judoka recognizes the attack too late and starts losing position backward because of the ouchi-gari attack, her only way out is to sweep with the attacked leg even while going down. In both of these cases, the judoka has been put in a position where the opponent's attack has progressed to a level where she needs to be careful. In other words, in order to counter, you must "let" the opponent attack to a certain degree that can often be close to getting thrown. "Allowing" an attack so that you can counter intentionally makes for exciting judo, but it is heart-stopping from a defensive point of view.

Two critical elements are necessary for countering. First, you must recognize the opponent's attack early; and, second, you must be able to react quickly and re-attack with the appropriate counter technique. The following are common counters for strong lines of defense.

Step Over → Kosoto-Gake

The defender (tori) goes with the force of the throw (tai-otoshi). The tori steps over the uke's leg and hooks the uke's heel, drawing his or her foot in the direction of the toe.

The uke attacks with tai-otoshi.

The tori steps over the uke's right leg, evading the tai-otoshi throw. The uke's extended leg is vulnerable for kosoto-gake.

For a strong kosoto-gake attack, the tori hooks with the heel of the foot and reaps it toward his body. The tori uses the right arm to push the uke's upper body back while the left arm pulls down.

Hop Around in Front → Ura-Nage

This counter uses the uke's attacking force against himself or herself. The tori uses centrifugal force against the uke as he or she swings around in front of the uke, yet holds on to the uke with both arms.

The uke attacks with seoi-nage. The tori turns by lifting the right leg around the uke's body.

The tori hops around so he is off the uke's hip and his feet can be planted on the mat. The tori stays low by bending the knees. If the tori cannot grip the uke's belt with the left arm, the tori should pull the uke tight.

The tori lifts and arches backward to throw the uke over with ura-nage.

Kata-Guruma → Crank Counter

The crank is one counter for kata-guruma but the other is to sprawl or throw the legs back or away from the tori. Another counter is to keep the sleeve hand of the uke down.

The uke enters with kata-guruma. The tori reacts by locking the hands and lifting the uke's left arm.	The tori steps behind the uke's right leg while straightening up and extending the uke's left arm.	The tori lowers toward the mat by blocking the uke's legs while countering the uke backward to the mat. The tori keeps contact while following the uke down to the mat to prevent the uke from turning while being thrown.

Hiza-Guruma → Kuchiki-Taoshi Counter

Many judo competitors rely on these kind of techniques which could be called ko-waza (minor techniques). Some fighters rely entirely on these "nickel and dime" throws which many pundits call "koka judo." However, in close matches, these can make the difference. Great skill is needed to pull these throws off at the high level.

The uke attacks with hiza-guruma.

The tori counters the hiza-guruma by grabbing the uke's leg with his right hand.

The tori moves with the throw, keeping the leg and pushing with the left hand straight backward. The tori keeps the leg as long as possible and falls with the uke to counter.

Tomoe-Nage → Cartwheel Escape

This technique is a novel way of escaping the tomoe-nage. It is also an enjoyable way to practice the throw without throwing the uke. Care must be shown to practice the cartwheel first to avoid injury.

The uke attacks with tomoe-nage.

The tori starts freeing the left hand so it can be placed down on the mat.

The tori cartwheels out of the throw. The tori should extend the body so he can land on the feet instead of bending the body, which makes it more difficult to avoid landing on one's back or side.

Uchi-Mata → Te-Guruma Counter

This technique was a popular counter that Phil Takahashi used in many competitions. It was taught to Phil by his father, Masao, in the early '70s. In this technique uke's attempt at uchi-mata is thwarted by tori's jigotai (defensive posture). Tori picks uke high to throw him over.

The tori lowers the body while reaching from behind high onto the uke's right leg.

The tori lifts with the arms while using the body to pop the uke off the mat. The tori clears uke's sweeping leg (right) out from between his. The tori must lift the uke's support leg (left) off the mat before trying to throw.

The tori quickly moves in front with the left hip to throw the uke over.

Uchi-Mata-Sukashi

After a lot of practice, you can read the uke's attack and evade his or her uchi-mata. This is done by side stepping and coinciding with the uke's momentum throw with a circular movement of the hands.

a The tori anticipates the uke to attack with uchi-mata.

b To prevent getting swept, the tori shifts weight onto the right leg so he can move the left leg away. The tori turns the left knee in, bringing the leg as close as possible to the right leg to eliminate an attack area for uchi-mata.

c The tori uses the momentum of the uke's throw to counter with uchi-mata-sukashi.

Uchi-Mata → Yoko-Guruma Counter

This technique follows the judo principle of yielding with the force and wheeling underneath to throw the attacker. Close contact is important throughout the whole technique.

Once contact is made, your block is successful. As the tori moves in with uchi-mata, the tori instantly swings around in front, wheeling under the uke as he shoots his leg between his leg, maintaining close contact until he is thrown over.

As the uke attacks with uchi-mata, the tori grips the uke's waist with the left hand and readies to counter.	The tori turns to the front, shooting the right leg through the uke's stance. The tori floats over the uchi-mata leg (the uke's right leg) to turn quickly to face the uke while rolling into the throw.	The tori uses the uke's momentum from the uchi-mata attack to continue into yoko-guruma by throwing while going to his back.

Physical Preparation and Weight Control

CHAPTER

8

Judo is a demanding sport because it utilizes a variety of physical components. You must be strong, have good aerobic endurance, and be quick in your attack and defense. It is difficult to quantify the exact contribution of a physical component in a match, partly because of individual differences among fighters and the various strategies that a match creates. In no particular order, the following physical components are important:

- *Strength.* Strength is important for moving your body quickly and against a resisting opponent in numerous positions, such as gripping, attacking, and defending. Strength is important in both standing (tachi-waza) and ground fighting (ne-waza).

- *Aerobic conditioning (with oxygen).* Matches are five minutes in length, so aerobic endurance is necessary. Aerobic conditioning aids in recovery between matches, especially when you have to fight in numerous matches over the tournament day.

- *Anaerobic conditioning (without oxygen).* Explosive movements in attack and defense require short powerful bursts of activity that may last a few seconds. Sustained high-intensity activity, such as gripping, taxes the lactic-acid energy system in the arms.

- *Flexibility.* Judo techniques such as uchi-mata demand flexibility as do the numerous movements in judo that involve rotation and twisting actions.

- *Agility.* Agility is required for both attack and defense and for moving quickly and gracefully in different directions: forward and back, side to side, and in circular motions.

- *Balance.* The key to judo tachi-waza lies in breaking the uke's balance. But also, it is important to develop specific balance for varying judo movements and actions, such as attacking, defending, and countering that may involve balancing on one leg and sweeping with the other.

It is rare for a judoka to have all these physical components at high levels. Physical components are only one factor in the makeup of a judo competitor. Psychological factors, such as toughness, confidence, and commitment, are also important. And match tactics play a significant role because they relate to what is likely the most important factor—technique.

TYPES OF TRAINING

The rules of judo elicit the kind of training you need to undergo. For example, tachi-waza is emphasized over ne-waza so you must train for the quick, explosive actions that standing judo entails. Prolonged ne-waza is rarely seen in today's judo, so emphasis on training for ne-waza would not be a wise choice or time well spent.

Even small modifications, especially to sport rules, elicit changes to training prescription. For example, at the Tokyo Olympics in 1964, final matches in judo were much longer at 15 minutes than the 5-minute finals of today. The shorter match time allows for different physical components and energy systems to come into play. Now, you need more power and less aerobic stamina, and the rules demand that you execute explosive (anaerobic) action.

Training in various physical components will help you to adapt to the possible levels of fatigue you can experience during a match. Almost every judoka has felt the burning sensation in the arms from lactic-acid buildup and exhaustion from the high levels of activity demanded over a five-minute match period. You must train to prepare for these outcomes through various training methods.

Fighting the Line (Kake Shobu)

One of the traditional training methods was "fighting the line" (a method still used but not as common today). A top fighter would fight a lineup of lower-ranked judoka (5 to 10 judoka) one by one. After scoring an ippon, the fighter would go on to the next partner and repeat until finished. This training method is demanding aerobically and anaerobically. But, because of the uncertainty of how the fights develop and end, it is difficult with this method to predict the type of physical training you will engage in and therefore train.

What this method does test, however, are the many necessary components that you will encounter in a tournament. Its design encourages going for ippon (attacking judo), simulates a competitive environment, and subjects you to pressure. Ray Takahashi remembers watching Hiroshi Nakamura, 8th Dan and Olympic judo coach for Canada, fighting a line: "I was about eleven or twelve years old, and I remember vividly seeing Nakamura fight a line of about ten fighters, and he threw them all for ippon!"

Aerobic Training

Aerobic training improves the aerobic, or cardiovascular, system so the body can work for long periods of time at submaximal intensities. Matches in judo demand good aerobic endurance. A judoka who is aerobically fit will be able to work harder throughout the match. As well, the ability to recover between matches will be enhanced with better aerobic fitness.

Aerobic training should be the base of all training for judo. Aerobic training can only be accomplished by working hard and long enough to make you breathe hard and break a sweat. Aerobic training can include low-intensity activity over long periods of time or higher-intensity periods repeated over and over, as in interval-type training. Aerobic training also prepares the body physically for the actions in judo by toughening ligaments, tendons, and connective tissue that help reduce injury.

Your aerobic system is measured by calculating your $\dot{V}O_2max$, defined as the maximum volume of oxygen uptake that can be used by the working muscles over a period of time, taking into consideration your weight. A higher $\dot{V}O_2max$ is better and means one can utilize more oxygen to supply energy. Aerobic exercise predominates after approximately two minutes of exercise. Endurance athletes such as marathon runners have high $\dot{V}O_2max$ values averaging around 70 milliliters per kilogram per minute (ml/kg/min), whereas an untrained individual scores 35 to 40 ml/kg/min. Judoka average around 50 ml/kg/min, which indicates that not only is the aerobic component important, but also an emphasis must be placed on anaerobic training and strength elements. A general guide to improving your aerobic capacity is to engage in activity in which you breathe hard enough to raise your heart rate to submaximal levels (60 percent and higher) for a minimum of 30 minutes. This training taxes the body and forces it to make adaptations so one can utilize more oxygen and use it more efficiently. If your activity is below the minimum, your body will not adapt, and you get no increase in stamina.

Strength Training

In any sport, strength is important. Judo is no exception, and strength is considered to be one of the most important physical components needed. The key is to incorporate strength in your technical abilities. Some judoka are exceptionally strong, but they do not use their strength effectively in their judo. Other judoka emphasize strength over technical aspects, which hinders their potential for full judo development. Some, mostly judo traditionalists, believe that strength is not vital to "good" judo. But, whatever the case, it is clear that the modern competitive judoka must be strong for his or her weight, especially if all other factors are equal, such as his or her technical abilities.

Some hold the view that children should not start strength training until they have finished growing. This view is a myth. There is evidence that supports the notion that strength training for children as young as 12 years of age is safe and beneficial if done correctly. For other populations, such as the elderly, strength training is extremely important because a lack of strength hinders them even in everyday living as they increase in age, more so than any other physical component.

Strength training is often viewed as lifting weights only. But, any exercise that overcomes resistance is a form of strength training. In judo, certain exercises and activities can be forms of strength training, such as a randori session where you work against the resistance of your uke. The problem with acquiring strength through judo techniques, although the most ideal method, is that strength training exercises must be done to exhaustion or near exhaustion, and be replicated over and over again in some systematic way to achieve optimal results. Training to exhaustion often compromises the quality of the technique itself, which can be more detrimental from a learning perspective and increases the risk in terms of injury.

Countless programs offer strength training, and many can be quite sophisticated. For example, bodybuilders have developed specific programs to increase muscle size. Olympic lifters have the goal to lift as much weight as possible through certain exercises, such as the clean and jerk, which requires speed, power, and technique. Athens Olympic weightlifting champion, Reza Zadeh (Iran), had a physique quite different from that of a bodybuilder. He was a huge man, weighing 353 pounds at 6 feet, 1 inch, with considerable girth and did not possess the muscular definition of a bodybuilder. His training allowed him to achieve status as the strongest man, lifting 1,040 pounds combining two lifts, the clean and jerk lift and the snatch. Bodybuilders, however, appear to be stronger but actually do not possess the absolute strength despite their greater muscular size.

Keep in mind that strength training is a supplemental activity to judo. You cannot spend the hours and hours necessary to improve strength that Olympic lifters do because your priority is to devote time to specific judo training. As well, strength training must gel with the type of judo training you are doing so that both can be effective to accomplish your ultimate goal of improving performance.

Many theories on weight training can be found, just as there are different methods for learning judo. The approach given here to weight training, therefore, is a simplistic approach that will provide you knowledge to engage in weight training for judo. Strength exercises should be multijoint and target large muscle groups. Four different strength types are categorized as follows (see table 8.1; V. Nolte. 2004. Adapted from course material from Kinesiology 410a Introduction to Coaching, School of Kinesiology. University of Western Ontario, London, Canada):

1. Power: Characterized by short, explosive movements largely trained by activation of the neuromuscular system in the body. Integrates maximum strength and speed.

2. Maximum strength: Develops relative strength (strength in relation to body weight).

3. Base training: Ideal for improving overall strength, which will lead to increased muscle size.

4. Strength–endurance: Combines strength and endurance. Helps in repeated or prolonged movements against a given resistance.

Table 8.1—Types of Strength Training					
Name	Load	Number of repetitions	Number of sets	Characteristics	Other names
Power	90-100%	1-3	4-5	Need full recovery between sets—up to 4 minutes. Use spotter because of maximum lifts. Need strength base first.	Neuromuscular training
Maximum strength	80-85%	5-7	3-5	Combination of power and base training.	Efficiency training
Base training	70-80%	8-12	3-5	Good for base development and overall strength.	Hypertrophy, bodybuilding method (increase in muscle size)
Strength–endurance	50-70%	+15	3-5	Can be used in circuit training. Taxes heart rate and lactic-acid system. Time between sets can be reduced to 1-3 minutes.	Lactic acid, muscular endurance

Load: Percentage based on 1RM. For example, 80% of RM of 200 lbs = 160 lbs.

Number of repetitions: Based on repetition maximum (RM). That is, 12RM is the amount one can lift 12 times. A maximum lift is 1RM.

Number of sets: If one lifts 80% load (160 lbs) 12 times in a row lifting equals one set of 12 reps.

Adapted from Nolte, V.

You can improve strength without gaining weight and developing muscle size. This consideration is particularly important for some judoka who need to stay within a certain weight class. Simply being strong or stronger may not improve performance in judo. For maximum benefits you must apply strength to a specific technique and develop specific strength in actions of the muscles that are used in performing techniques.

The load, or resistance or amount lifted, is an important variable because it determines the kind of strength training in which one engages. A light load, below 60 percent of your maximum, would be too light to achieve significant strength gains but would be good to train strength–endurance, where a buildup in lactic acid can be generated by higher repetitions (higher than 15). Conversely, a high load of 95 percent of your maximum could only be lifted one to three times, for example. This latter type of prescription favors power development, in which the nervous system learns to fire quickly to recruit and activate muscle fibers. Interestingly, high-load, low repetition training for power is not as conducive to muscle mass gain as many believe. Hypertrophy, where the muscle increases in size, is best produced when the muscle targeted is overloaded with a higher number of repetitions, usually between 8 to 12 per set, and totaling more than 40 repetitions over three to five sets (base training method). Because in high-load or power training the total repetitions is fewer, hypertrophy doesn't occur. Instead, in high-load training, there is a recruitment of muscle fibers by nervous-system adaptation. In strength–endurance training, lactic acid builds up, which really isn't a true form of strength development, but is important in judo because of the lactic-acid buildup that occurs in the arms and muscles over a five-minute match.

TRAINING VARIABLES

By altering the intensity, speed, and difficulty level of an activity, training methods will produce different training results. Generally, training objectives should improve one or both components of physical or technical training. That is, depending on the design of the training, you will acquire a physical training effect, technical development, or a combination of both.

Intensity

Intensity is a measure of how hard you are working. Some actions in a judo match, such as a throwing attempt, require high or full intensity for a very short duration (one to three seconds). Over the course of a match you cannot continuously perform at the anaerobic level because you will fatigue after one or two minutes at full intensity. Depending on the actions that occur in a match, the intensity changes so you must train for the various intensities that may occur.

The competitive judoka must strike a balance between the aerobic and anaerobic energy systems. You must be able to engage in high-intensity actions that require power and speed (for example, attacking or countering a throw) and have the endurance to last the duration of the match, recover from it, and fight up to five times over the tournament day. A common measure of aerobic intensity is to work at a percentage of your maximum heart rate (for example, 75 to 85 percent). Working above this rate (for example, 90 to 100 percent) requires greater effort and cannot be sustained for more than one to two minutes, at which time a buildup in lactic acid in the muscles will inhibit your ability to work. Training your energy systems for judo is challenging not only because it involves training a combination of both the anaerobic and aerobic systems but also because you must incorporate technical training along with tactics (see table 8.2).

Table 8.2—Physical Training: Altering Outcomes			
Exercise period (minutes)	**Rest (minutes)**	**Description**	**Objectives**
1 × 20 minutes = 20 minutes	No rest periods	70% sub-maximal intensity (of maximum heart rate). Judoka is able to engage in judo with periodic spurts of high-intensity attacks and actions.	Aerobic (base) conditioning Pacing
4 × 5-minute periods = 20 minutes	5 minutes	85% high intensity	Matchlike conditions Improve ability to work at anaerobic threshold level
20 × 1-minute periods = 20 minutes	2 minutes	90-100% full intensity	Develop intensity Anaerobic and high-power aerobic conditioning

Let's say you will engage in 20 minutes of randori. By altering work and rest periods, randori training elicits different outcomes from a physical training perspective. A different training effect can be created in one long 20-minute randori session compared to one session that is broken into 20 1-minute periods. In the 20-minute continuous session, you would need to pace yourself and work at approximately 70 percent of aerobic capacity. Although matches do not last 20 minutes in length, this type of training is important for developing an aerobic base. From a technical standpoint, it is valuable to train for long, continuous periods so that you and your partner have the time to develop your attacks and use tactics. Training in 20 one-minute periods, you would be able to work at a higher intensity within each one-minute period—almost at 100-percent intensity. With a 2-minute rest period, you would be able to recover enough to repeat this intensity, and over the 20-minute work time, this type of work is very physically demanding.

Increased Speed

The speed of attack and how fast you can move when entering into a throw are important. You must get your body into position as quick as possible before you can mount an offense and develop your speed of attack in the precise movements required by the technique. When practicing, therefore, be sure to train with high intensity because speed is a component of power. Similarly, in uchikomi training (once the technical movements are learned) you can increase the speed of the repetitions to achieve two main objectives: Engage in specific physical training, and train the body to automate the action of the throw.

To develop specific physical conditioning, alter the speed, duration, and number of repetitions. For example, fewer but higher-intensity repetitions with longer rest intervals are good for developing power. Longer intervals (for example, three-minute periods) executed with submaximal intensity produce greater aerobic conditioning and increase endurance in the muscles used in the actions of the throw.

Difficulty

With increased intensity, the ability to perform technique well decreases. The difficulty is being able to work hard enough and still be able to perform the techniques correctly. There is little value in increasing intensity if you are then unable to perform technique properly because you are too exhausted. Yet, you cannot obtain the desired training effect if you cannot acquire the intensity. Consider a top competitor who cannot push herself hard enough because of a lack of good partners. Another difficulty is regulating the intensity in randori consistently at the level desired. Randori is dynamic and full of action, which makes it difficult to control. (This is why off-mat conditioning is needed.)

TRAINING FOR COMPETITION

Training for competition requires a systematic approach that is aimed at preparing you to perform your best in a tournament. If you know you want to peak at a particular tournament or time of year, then your physical and mental preparation can be better planned to maximize your performance. Peaking can be described as bringing together physical and mental factors so you are able to perform maximally at a specified time period. Peaking is also needed in judo because the combative nature of it requires time for recovery and rest from competition and daily training.

Training programs can be quite detailed, although this detail does not always guarantee optimal performance. Training programs can last several years, such as quadrennial plans cycled around the Olympic Games or a four-year university program. Shorter, seasonal plans could be yearly or part of a year such as those mirroring an academic year.

The ability to perform in tournaments involves many interacting factors, which makes it difficult to establish a single ideal training method for judo. Many examples can be cited where a developing nation brings in an expert from a world judo power only to find the coaching and training did not produce the desired results. What works in one system may not work in another. Simply put, numerous factors must be taken into account to design the optimal program that can best bring out an individual's or a team's efforts. Most important, judoka must buy into the program by following through with it. There are many good training programs on paper, but they have little value if they are not followed and believed in.

A training plan can be thought of as a theoretical process where you follow certain steps over a period of time. The plan should provide direction to achieve a particular goal that is best suited to you. Unfortunately, most judoka are not privileged to have a personalized training program because most training or practice sessions at a dojo must cater to the entire group, not the individual. The challenge of the instructor is to weigh the needs of individuals, especially those who may be elite competitors, and the needs of others who may comprise the bulk of the class (and who may also be paying members). The instructor who aims to develop competitive fighters, however, would need to develop a training plan so training is not haphazard in its approach. Because of judo's individual nature (individual sport versus team sport), judo has an inherent advantage in meeting the needs of individual judoka to a certain degree.

Consider the Demands of Competitive Judo

The first consideration in developing a training plan is to understand the demands of judo and the level to which you have risen. Knowing the demands of judo means knowing what physical, technical, psychological, and tactical factors are involved in the sport. Having the knowledge and being able to quantify the demands of judo will then provide the direction to determine what you need to focus on in training.

This analysis will establish a starting point. There is no sense in starting an advanced power weight training routine if you do not have the physical starting base or have never lifted weights before, or power is not yet needed at your particular level. Likewise, you would not want to work on certain technical drills if you have not yet mastered basic techniques. The retrospective analysis will provide information on what to focus.

Accept Environmental Limitations

Environmental limitations on training include factors such as training partners, facilities, the support system, and individual finances. For example, you should not design a training plan based on five mat practices a week if circumstances do not allow you to attend more than three practices a week. In this case, environmental limitations affect the amount of training you can participate in realistically. Some judoka never reach their full potential because they just are not in the proper environment to do well (some, however, do not reach their full potential because they lack a solid work ethic).

Set Achievement Goals

The training plan should state your goals clearly to provide you with motivation and direction. For example, you may have the goal of achieving the next belt level. You may also have a competitive goal of placing in a series of tournaments or being able to perform certain techniques in competition. The goal may even be to beat a certain opponent. Goals can be short term, or those that can be achieved earlier in the season, and be used to measure progress toward a larger long-term goal.

Develop a Training Plan

A training program is like a recipe. Not all recipes will satisfy everyone's tastes so adjustments to them are necessary. Chefs, like coaches, will follow a basic recipe but must be flexible to make changes to it when needed. Because so many variables in judo are out of your control, the training plan should be a guideline that allows for flexibility. For example, what happens if you get sick or injured? Obviously, you would need to make adjustments to the training plan and hope that you will be able to "work back in" after some recovery time.

Training plans in sports that involve objective, measurable factors, such as time and distance, can be very detailed. Some training plans can be illustrated in a calendar format, graph, or periodization chart. The difficulty in designing a similar training plan for judo is that so many factors need to be considered, such as the following:

- Variances in technical ability, athletic ability (talent), and experience
- Physical limitations, history of injuries, and the potential health risks
- Strategic and tactical considerations
- Psychological demands of competition
- Individual learning styles

Here are some basic steps to follow in designing a training program:

- Identify important dates. It is important to identify the tournament dates that will occur in the season. The last tournament will usually be the major tournament where you will peak. You may find clusters of competitions occur together, indicating a competitive period. Slower periods, for example, during the school exam period or over the winter holidays, can be identified as "transition" periods. Other events such as training sessions and camps should also be noted. Generally, the length of the season from start to finish is established with tournament dates in place.

- Determine the number of training sessions. The number of training sessions per week will provide the overall volume of training in which you will engage. For example, before a competitive period you will need to train more frequently, getting in daily mat workouts. Elite athletes may be on the mat as much as twice a day prior to a tournament.

A number of weeks put together (usually three to eight) represents the time frame where significant improvements can be made, often called a "macrocycle." A macrocycle may have a specific objective such as to increase strength or develop basic techniques. Weekly sessions, or "mesocycles," are easy to plan because the calendar year lends itself well to fit, and we typically think in terms of weeks. A daily session is termed a "microcycle" and would involve the practice content to achieve the objective within the larger cycle. See table 8.3, which summarizes recommended training activities for each phase of the yearly training plan.

TERMS USED IN A TRAINING PLAN
- Microcycle—daily plan
- Mesocycle—weekly plan
- Macrocycle—number of weeks (usually three to eight)
- Phases or seasons
  - Preparatory phase—preseason; can be further subdivided into general and specific preparation.
  - Competitive phase—in-season; when the bulk of tournaments occur.
  - Transition phase—off-season; a recovery phase associated with active recuperation, both physically and psychologically.

Training phase	Judo	Strength	Conditioning	Mental	Timing	Weeks
					Table 8.3—Yearly Training Plan	
Preparatory (general)	1. Develop major standing and ground techniques. 2. Establish primary grip.	1. Train max strength and muscular endurance.	1. Train aerobic.	1. Establish seasonal goals. 2. Train relaxation skills.	July 1 to Sept 8	10
Preparatory (specific)	1. Refine major techniques. 2. Develop minor techniques to be used in combination with major techniques. 3. Refine gripping skills (e.g., breaking grips, attacking off the grip).	1. Train max strength and muscular endurance.	1. Train aerobic. 2. Begin training anaerobic lactic.	1. Maintain relaxation skills. 2. Train skills in visualization, activation, and positive self-talk.	Sept 9 to Nov 3	8
Precompetitive	1. Refine major and minor techniques. 2. Develop a leg or "surprise" attack. 3. Emphasize competitive tactics in training—line work, defending a lead, tactical gripping.	1. Maintain max strength and muscular endurance. 2. Train speed-strength (power).	1. Maintain aerobic. 2. Train anaerobic lactic. 3. Begin training anaerobic alactic.	1. Refine all mental training skills, and apply them to specific competitive goals.	Nov 4 to Jan 5	9

(continued)

Table 8.3 *(continued)*

Training phase	Judo	Strength	Conditioning	Mental	Timing	Weeks
Main competitive	1. Evaluate the athletes' performance, and analyze their competition. 2. Make the necessary adjustments to their judo base to maximize the chances of success in competition.	1. Maintain max strength and muscular endurance. 2. Train and maintain speed-strength. 3. Taper with circuit training.	1. Maintain training of all three energy systems. 2. Train anaerobic alactic.	1. Evaluate and reestablish seasonal goals. 2. Execute, evaluate, and refine mental training routine.	Jan 6 to April 13 Taper: April 14 to May 7	14 / taper 3
Transition (off-season)	1. Judo (1-2x/week) for fun, or take a complete rest if desired.	1. Maintain max strength with 1 weight training session/week.	1. Maintain aerobic fitness through regular activity other than judo.	1. Begin to think about goal setting for next season.	May 10 to June 30	7

Dates are based on the following competition examples:

* Age Category
Senior elite (adults)
*Major Competitions
Rendez-vous Canada: October 18
Ontario Open: November 22 to 23
Kamloops Open: February 7
Pacific International Sr.: February 21
Senior Nationals: May 8 to 9
*Minor Competitions
BC Championships: October 18
Burnaby: December 6

Vancouver Island Open: January 17
Spirit International: February 28
Okanagan Valley Open: April 3
*Training Camps
Xmas Camp: December 27 to 30
Team Training Sessions: January 18, February 8 and 22
Senior Nationals Preparation: April 17 to 18
*Training Phases
July 1, 2003 to June 30, 2004

Contributed by Renee Hock, B.C. Judo, Canada, 2003-04.

DECREASING BODY WEIGHT

Physical adaptations to training take time; typically, significant gains occur in four to six weeks. As you become more physically fit so too does your ability to train at higher intensities and to increase the volume of training. As a result, your body weight may change while you are developing a greater awareness of your physical abilities and makeup. Body weight is used to differentiate competitors along with age and rank, so it becomes an important factor if you are going to compete. Usually, your aim will be to either reduce, maintain, or increase your body weight.

It is an advantage for you to be heavier (and stronger) than your opponent. This advantage is why many elite judo competitors have little body fat relative to their muscle mass. It would be a disadvantage to carry excess weight if it were body fat because body fat offers little, if any, benefit to the fighter. The ideal would be to weigh near the upper limit of the weight class versus the bottom. Making weight refers to engaging in the process to make a specific weight division, typically by reducing weight. For example, a judoka who weighs 74 kilograms (163 pounds) would likely consider losing 1 kilogram (about 2 pounds) to make the 73-kilogram (160-pound) weight class to be placed at the upper limit for that grouping rather than competing in the 81-kilogram weight class where opponents could theoretically be 7 kilograms (15 pounds) heavier. Even in the long term, it is much easier to lose 1 kilogram than it is to gain 7 kilograms of muscle and bone.

Absolute strength, or being as strong as you can be irrespective of your body weight, is especially relevant in the heavyweight class where there is no upper limit. However, it is ideal if you have a high strength ratio per unit of body weight; that is, if you are stronger than your opponent while sharing the same body weight. It is a distinct advantage to be stronger than your opponent.

Effective weight control will allow you to train and compete at a body weight that maximizes your physical conditioning for a particular weight class. Learning to control your weight takes time because the body must make adaptations to the training process. If you are in good condition, you are also better able to respond to weight-reduction methods than someone who is not physically fit.

The judoka often looks for ways to gain an advantage as a competitor. A study on the weight-loss practices of judoka by Dave Coles. (The Weight-loss Practices of Judoka. D. Coles. 2001. Judo Information Site. http://www.judoinfo.com/research12.htm) revealed that of 165 judoka surveyed (males, $n = 123$, average age 29 years and females, $n = 42$, average age 22 years), 86 percent reported that they intentionally lost weight in order to make their fighting weight. This high percentage indicates that the majority of judoka are attempting to gain an advantage by reducing their body weight. Unfortunately, too many judoka find themselves continually reducing their body weight to gain an advantage even when it is unnecessary. More important, continued weight loss, especially if pursued in an unsafe manner, can be unhealthy if the weight to be lost is unrealistic or if the method used is inappropriate.

Teenage males and females must be careful about losing weight, especially those in the lighter weight classes. Generally, those in heavier weight classes lose more weight with the same amount of work. Females and males who are still growing have a greater tendency to rebound to a heavier weight after their dieting is finished, particularly if the weight loss was done very quickly or improperly (i.e., fasting). Continual "crash" dieting can affect one's metabolism negatively by slowing it down, and consequently making it easier to gain, and harder to lose, weight.

Clearly, certain groups of people should not engage in weight loss. Children and those still growing (for example, teenagers during a growth spurt) should avoid excessive and continual practice of weight loss because their bodies are still developing. For those judoka who are generally healthy, the question is why they really want to lose weight. This question needs to be answered because too often judoka believe the obvious solution to gaining an advantage is to lose weight. However, the process or method of losing weight can be counterproductive and affect one's training and one's health negatively. More often than not, judoka should redirect their focus from losing weight to improving other aspects of their judo, such as their technique, to gain an advantage over their opponents.

In some cases, weight loss is warranted, particularly if you belong (given your height and size) in a lower weight class. If you are concerned about your weight, get an accurate scale so that you can be sure that you make weight with a small margin and are not too much underweight. Be aware that your weight will fluctuate during the day. Fluctuations in body weight that occur during the day are usually a result of water-weight loss, a result of eating, and bowel movements. Also, after a hard practice, you can lose two to four pounds through perspiration alone, so these fluctuations are impermanent and normal. With some record keeping, you can determine weight loss caused by perspiration, respiration, and other bodily functions. You should never attempt to make weight at a peak tournament at a lower class if you have not done it earlier in the season. It is important to develop experience under tournament conditions or to even know if weight loss is the right thing to do. Whatever the case, you can use several methods to achieve the preferred weight. These methods are discussed next.

Fat-Reducing Method

Reducing body fat is the most ideal method of weight loss because fat has little value to the judoka other than body padding. Body fat will not come into play in a tournament even as an energy source because a match does not demand it (too short and intense) and you will have time between matches to refuel with liquid or food.

Weight reduction in its simplest equation can be expressed by burning more energy (calories) than one is ingesting (through food). It is preferable to reduce your weight slowly over a long duration because the weight reduction can be implemented over the training process. You would not need then to drastically reduce your weight at the last minute for competition, and your weight loss would be focused on body-fat loss. Losing body fat requires discipline and healthy eating habits. You can obtain considerable information on nutrition and the needs of the athlete through the Internet, your public library, and various organizations. Be careful, however, about information when its purpose is to sell you something.

You should have healthy nutritional habits that will allow for enough energy to repair and build the body. Avoid excess, nutrient-poor calories. Instead, eat a variety of nutrient-dense foods in quantities that you require for your particular stage of growth and development.

The best way to reduce body fat is to increase the amount of exercise. It takes about one week to lose up to about two pounds (about one kilogram) of fat safely. To do this, expend more calories than you ingest, where a net loss of 3,500 calories is required for losing one pound (about ½ kilogram) of body weight (fat and the associated tissue). Once you lose fat weight, you can keep it off easily by maintaining the energy balance (calories eaten equal calories burned).

It is difficult to determine the caloric cost of judo because it is so dynamic in nature, and it is difficult to regulate intensity and its actions. Other activities allow for calorie cost to be determined more easily. For example, running can be maintained at constant effort, and thus calorie cost can be easily measured on a treadmill under controlled conditions (in a laboratory). It is estimated that one hour of running expends 1,000 calories (about 100 calories per mile depending on body weight and speed). The calorie cost of some dynamic activities has been measured; for example, wrestling has been estimated to expend approximately 1,200 calories per hour. It would seem, therefore, that judo could be considered comparable using around 1,200 calories for randori activity. Using these values of energy expenditure, a judoka could lose one pound of fat in one week by engaging in randori three times for one hour. The energy expenditure is calculated as follows: 3 days × 1,200 calories = 3,600 total calories (where 1 pound of body weight = 3,500 calories).

Given this formula, if you needed to lose three pounds to make a lower weight class, it would take you three weeks to lose three pounds. Therefore, over an extended period you can easily lose three pounds of fat permanently, a desirable outcome. But, what if you had to lose the weight faster or did not have three fat pounds to lose from your body? If you still wanted to lose the three pounds in one week, you would have to increase the exercise volume to the equivalent of nine randori sessions (three practices times three days per week). Exercising this much may be difficult for some, especially because this increase in exercise would occur in addition to the normal training routine. Alternatively, you run or swim between practices to burn off weight as well as increase your cardiovascular fitness.

Dehydration Method

Making weight can also be accomplished by the controversial and often dangerous dehydration method. Dehydration methods are particularly taxing and are an extreme method of reducing weight. It should be clearly stated that dehydration methods are not condoned as a method of weight loss. The rationale of providing information on these methods is to educate the reader on practices that are being used. In some cases, the dehydration method is necessary if the elite athlete has no excess body fat to lose. In weight-class sports such as judo, wrestling, and boxing, dehydration is commonplace. There are many other sports where body weight is a factor in performance, such as gymnastics; long-distance running; and even horseracing, where the jockey undergoes extreme weight-reduction methods so the horse carries less weight and will then run faster. Readers should understand that only a small percentage of judoka (elite competitors) should engage in these types of practices.

The dehydration weight-loss method works as follows. Let's say you want to make a certain weight and you are three pounds too heavy. You decide to "sweat it off" rather than reduce body fat. You would engage in activity for one to two hours and keep active so that you are constantly sweating over the duration of the workout. If you wear more clothing such as a sweat top underneath your jacket you can sweat more although you should be careful it does not prevent you from practicing judo. You would not drink during this time, and the sweat you lose in the workout will reflect the weight you have lost (although, some "water weight" is also lost through respiration). Once you weigh in, you can then rehydrate with the intention of regaining all of the water weight lost. The weigh-in usually occurs in the morning prior to the tournament with at least two hours before the start of the first match. The judoka must understand that excessive dehydration will affect physical performance (e.g., aerobic endurance) and it would be wise to experiment before practice sessions so one knows how much weight can be lost by this method.

If you are dehydrating to lose weight, avoid carbohydrates, which increase the amount of water held in the body. Diuretics should be avoided. Although alcohol will cause you to lose water, and some people incorrectly believe that it helps them sleep, it should also be avoided because it affects the sense of balance long after other more obvious symptoms have disappeared.

The main advantage of the dehydration method is that it's fast. Also, you can get an immediate result from the effort of the weight-loss workout, whereas in the fat-reduction method, you need to wait days to see a change in body weight. With dehydration weight-loss methods, you could lose three pounds in one workout, whereas in the fat-reduction method, a week is required to lose the same amount. Although the quick results sound promising, dehydration methods create many disadvantages. Most are related to serious health risks. Others can affect performance. Fasting and fluid restriction usually accompany these methods and are typically maintained for 24 to 48 hours. Such restriction can have a negative effect on one's psychological well-being.

Heat-related conditions accompany dehydration reduction methods because you must raise your body temperature in order to sweat, which is actually a natural cooling mechanism. Dehydration becomes an issue in many sports, particularly those where sweating occurs over prolonged periods of time or in weight-class sports, such as judo and wrestling. In the sport of American football, many cases are reported every year of heat exhaustion and dehydration during summer practices (and complicated by players wearing heat-retaining equipment). According to the U.S. Catastrophic Sports Injury Research Center, 18 high school or college football players died of heat-related causes over a seven-year period from 1995 to 2002.

In 2001 the media focused on professional football lineman Korey Stringer of the Minnesota Vikings, who died during football practice after suffering heatstroke. Also in the United States, three college wrestlers died of dehydration complications while making weight in 1999. Their deaths prompted changes in NCAA (National Collegiate Athletic Association) rules and policies on weight reduction by participating wrestlers. Although judo is different from wrestling and football, judoka need to be concerned about dehydration and related conditions. Training sessions for the elite judoka can be physically demanding, and prolonged hard training in a hot, humid environment can lead to a high degree of sweat loss. These conditions are complicated with the wearing of a heavy judogi jacket and outdated, traditional training expectations of "toughing it out" by not taking water breaks during practice. Normally, heat exhaustion accompanies dehydration, and the combination can easily be triggered in weight-class sports. Although not normally a concern during typical training, you need to be especially wary of these conditions if you are practicing weight control for competition.

Fighting the Elements

Canadian Nicolas Gill not only had to fight a formidable opponent in Mario Sabino of Brazil at the 14th Pan American Games in Santo Domingo (2003) but also the hot and humid conditions. Gill, who has two Olympic medals, battled heat, humidity, and exhaustion that zapped him physically in the 100-kilogram (220 pounds) gold medal final. The Canadian press quoted him saying: "I started feeling sick, and my heartbeat was stuck and wouldn't go down anymore. It was frustrating because I didn't have the power I normally have and to lose like this, it's very frustrating." Environmental conditions exacerbated the grueling overtime match over his earlier Cuban opponent from which Gill could not recover, even after the Canadian medical staff pumped him full of fluids. Against Sabino, whom Gill had beaten previously and since in the Pan Am final, no amount of will and fight would save him from the effects of heat exhaustion and dehydration.

Extreme dehydration is dangerous and poses serious health risks including dizziness; nausea; and in extreme cases, even death. Thirst is the first sign that the body requires fluids and can trigger when the body is dehydrated at 1 percent. Symptoms of dehydration begin to emerge at around 2 to 3 percent, accompanied by a stronger thirst, loss of appetite, and a feeling of vague discomfort. At 5 percent dehydration one experiences apathy, lack of motivation, dizziness, and nausea. In a 10 percent dehydrated state, a person would be in serious trouble with the body systems starting to shut down. Circulatory insufficiency, decreased blood volume, and delirium set in. At 15 percent dehydration, the person experiences an inability to swallow. The person's vision becomes impaired and the skin is numb. Twenty percent dehydration is fatal.

Some judoka believe that dehydrating to make weight and then rehydrating immediately after weigh-ins will eliminate negative effects and they will return to normal levels prior to the first match. Unfortunately, the body does not respond quickly enough because the time period from weigh-in to the first match is inadequate for a full recovery. Furthermore, if weigh-ins are held the morning of the tournament, being dehydrated the night before will not allow a good night's sleep. Because of all of these serious concerns, it is important to minimize dehydration as a method of weight loss.

INCREASING BODY WEIGHT

An increase in body weight can occur for several reasons. If one ingests more energy (calories) than the body needs, the body stores the energy as body fat, which is then carried as extra weight. Excess body fat is not desirable in judo because rarely does fat provide any substantial advantage to the competitive judoka.

Natural growth and development is another reason for an increase in weight gain. This is especially true for teenagers who can grow significantly in height and weight during a growth spurt. Weight gain through natural growth and development should not be hindered, and individuals who are still growing should let nature take its course.

You can increase your muscle mass through strength training in which the muscles increase in size (hypertrophy). Gaining muscle weight that becomes permanent is actually difficult to do (you can, conversely, atrophy—that is, lose muscle through inactivity). You need to work hard, usually for at least six weeks and with the proper methods to see significant strength and hypertrophy gains. Sometimes it takes years to "grow" into a heavier weight class. Increasing muscle mass and strength is a good strategy if you are in the middle of your weight category, especially if you are still growing.

NUTRITIONAL TRAINING NEEDS

Weight control goes hand in hand with diet, and it makes sense that both must be considered for responsible training. You should be particularly sensitive to eating healthy if you are trying to reduce your weight. In today's society there are abundant food choices that, fortunately and unfortunately, you can choose from to supply your nutritional needs. It becomes more and more challenging to make wise food choices given the prevalence of fast-food restaurants and processed and convenience foods.

Once you invest seriously in training, you will need to pay more attention to weight control and nutritional needs, especially if you are competing. The essential food elements that are needed for the body to function are water, carbohydrates, protein, fat, vitamins, and minerals. Athletes need more energy (calories) because they are more active and burn off more calories than nonathletes. This means their bodies require higher levels of carbohydrate, which are the main source of immediate energy used during exercise.

Additional protein in the diet is important for the building and repair of muscle and tissue. The active judoka needs more protein than an inactive person because the activity of judo is demanding and utilizes many muscle groups. Eating some protein with carbohydrate will help your body to replenish energy stores more quickly. It is also important to allow your body an adequate amount of recovery time so that protein can work in your body to aid muscle and tissue repair after strenuous activity. Fluid replacement is equally critical during regular training sessions, especially when conditions are hot and humid as previously discussed. You would be well advised to drink "more than enough" in training because you can become dehydrated without realizing it.

A guideline for the amount of protein you should try to ingest per day is approximately 1.5 to 2 grams per kilogram of body weight. That means a judoka weighing 73 kilograms (about 160 pounds) would need approximately 110 to 146 grams of protein per day (3 ounces of meat or fish, which is about the size of a deck of cards, contain about 20 to 30 grams of protein). An overly high protein diet isn't advisable because it can damage the kidneys. Fat from healthy oils should represent approximately 20 percent of your total caloric intake, whereas carbohydrate should be the main source of calories, or about 65 percent. A diet low in carbohydrate will be insufficient to keep your glycogen levels (the fuel used by the body and stored in the liver and muscles) adequate for supplying the energy your body needs for hard training and competition.

NUTRITIONAL CONSIDERATIONS DURING A TOURNAMENT

Your body is subjected to certain nutritional demands during a competition. First, you must adequately recover from weigh-ins, and, second, you must be sure to acquire adequate energy requirements during the competition day.

Post-Weigh-In

The objective of the post-weigh-in meal is to replenish energy stores and fluids and to ensure that you are prepared to compete for the first match. Timing is important, and you should have a good indication of when your first match is scheduled because how and what you ingest will depend on when it is scheduled.

Some tournaments have "night-before" weigh-ins whereas others are "day-of." Night-before weigh-ins allow you to replenish energy stores over a longer period of time, which would be fortunate especially if you have been watching your weight. Morning-of weigh-ins allow for a short time period, usually from two to four hours, before you first compete. With such a short time period for recovery, it is important for you to replenish fluids and nutrients properly because a major concern is being able to digest food so that you are not fighting on a full stomach. Some examples of easily digested foods are rice, toast, noodles, baked potatoes, fruit, soup, and sandwiches. Avoid fatty meat, beans, and milk.

Tournament Day

Over the course of a competition day you will need adequate energy to engage in approximately five matches. It is essential therefore that you eat and drink during the day to replenish your energy stores. Typically, matches are spread out over the day, allowing for brief opportunities to snack and drink.

Eating during competition day is largely individual. That is, what is preferred for one judoka may not be good for another. Experience will dictate how you determine what is right for you. For example, one judoka may prefer eating a banana, another an orange. A typical North American diet will differ from an Asian or a European diet. A Japanese judoka may prefer rice whereas the North American may choose a pasta or bread product to replenish carbohydrate for energy.

You have an abundance of nutritional choices, and much will depend on experience (trial and error). You would be best advised however, not to experiment or try something drastically new on tournament day; instead test a new food or drink during training sessions over the season. You must remember that competition adds the element of stress that one typically does not experience during practice. During a tournament, food and drink choices must accomplish the needed functions of the body first and not be overridden by your preference for taste. The three objectives in choosing food and drinks on competition day are listed next:

- It should satisfy hunger and thirst.
- It should provide enough energy to compete throughout the day.
- It should replace fluids lost throughout the day.

Some judoka prefer not to eat at all or very little (preferring fluid replacement instead). Others may choose to eat small snacks throughout the day when time permits. A "liquid meal" such as a protein drink will be digested easier because fluids are emptied from the stomach quicker.

During competition day some common considerations include the following:

• Eat and drink things to which you are accustomed. Don't experiment during competition.

• Choose foods that are easily digestible. Stay away from high-fat, overly spicy, and greasy foods.

• Eat carbohydrate with protein. Avoid fat if possible. Although fat has more energy (calories) than carbohydrate it cannot be utilized as an immediate energy source during competition day. Obviously, you want to avoid foods that would be just dead weight in your body. This may mean that you should be careful what you eat a full day before weigh-in.

• Consider what you choose to eat and drink in terms of the timing of competition. This does not only mean leaving enough time for digestion before an upcoming match. But, also, the timing of ingesting foods is important so that the body can utilize the food as energy for upcoming matches. Eating immediately (within 15 minutes) following a match is best because the body is able to absorb nutrients faster when your metabolism is high.

• Be careful of the carbohydrate rebound effect. Too much sugar is not good. You can actually get tired from eating simple carbohydrate, such as a candy bar or other high-sugar foods or drinks. The body secretes insulin (a hormone produced by the pancreas) to regulate blood-sugar levels; too much sugar triggers high levels of insulin to be released that then cause an imbalance in blood sugar.

Avoid eating high concentrations of sugar within one hour of a match. However, if you time it properly the high sugar can be used immediately as energy for an upcoming match (within 10 minutes). Consuming high amounts of sugar is not recommended, however, because it is difficult to estimate the best time to consume carbohydrate and the amount needed to last throughout the next match.

• Drink plenty of fluids. The main objective of fluid replacement during the day of the tournament is to replace fluids lost through sweating and to provide energy for the working muscles. Therefore, fluid replacement is important for optimal recovery after weigh-ins and also to stay hydrated throughout the tournament day.

Evidence shows that dehydration affects physical performance negatively. Dehydration affects the electrolyte (salt) balance in the blood, which allows for the proper functioning of muscles and nerves. Generally, aerobic capacity is the ability of the body to use oxygen that is breathed so that the muscles are able to work at a high intensity over time. Dehydration impairs aerobic capacity, which creates strong negative implications. Dehydration decreases aerobic capacity in two main ways: the ability to endure the demands of the match and the ability to recover after a hard match. This loss becomes particularly important as a tournament progresses.

As mentioned earlier, excessive dehydration can impair performance and even imposes a health risk normally associated with drastic weight reduction. It is important to hydrate after weigh-ins as soon as possible. It takes approximately one hour for the body to absorb one liter of water, although absorption will occur faster if you are dehydrated. You should not "chug" fluid or drink as fast as you can as it may make you feel sick. Instead, drink in small quantities immediately after weigh-ins and regularly over the course of a few hours.

It is equally important to keep hydrated during the tournament day, especially in hot, humid conditions. Water remains the best-accepted fluid for rehydration. Water offers no energy or mineral replacement, however, something that you may require during the course of the tournament day. This is particularly true when you must prepare, warm up, and compete repeatedly up to four to six times over the day. As well, with relatively short periods of time for recovery, you may not be able to ingest food for energy consumption; hence, the need for sport drinks.

Energy drinks, many of which are now very popular, vary in their carbohydrate concentration and some provide protein as well. An optimal level is 5 to 8 percent sugar concentration. Fruit juices can contain 12 to 15 percent sugar and therefore should be diluted with water. Overconcentrated carbohydrate and electrolytes in fluid can slow and interfere with the absorption of water. Therefore, when mixing powdered energy drinks, be careful not to overconcentrate the mixture (often thought the more the better) as it could impede the proper absorption rate of water.

What you prefer and find agreeable is, again, largely individual in nature. Some judoka will avoid coffee the morning of a tournament whereas others feel it gives them a needed boost. Still others may avoid milk and products that have a thick or coating sensation to the throat. Carbonated drinks such as colas may upset the stomach and are high in sugar.

SUPPLEMENTS

The competitive judoka who is under great pressure to succeed will resort to almost any tactic, nutritional or otherwise, to gain an edge. There is also a trend to use food supplements to gain an advantage, and the industry gives the impression that athletes have special nutritional needs. Although the need for supplements is debatable, what can be emphasized is that sound nutrition through a balanced meal is the best advice, whether one is an elite competitor or recreational judoka. To use a judo analogy, you must learn and practice the basics before substituting with advanced and fancy techniques. In every book written by top fighters emphasis is placed on fundamental training; the same is true with regard to the fundamentals of eating a simple, balanced meal. Today, many supplements are available in retail stores and outlets that you may find enticing. Supplements for dieting, fat reduction, weight gain, and strength gain are readily available—but many of these have not been regulated, tested, or proven to be effective.

Many judoka believe there is a shortcut to being a champion, thinking that by taking a supplement it will give them a distinct advantage and their performance will improve. Others believe that supplements will make them healthier, change their body composition, and give them more energy. In fact, there is limited research to clearly indicate that dietary supplements can do these things and enhance athletic performance.

The benefits of sound nutrition and good eating habits cannot be overemphasized. The condoning of taking nutritional supplements must be addressed cautiously, even if only on a philosophical basis. The position supported in this book, therefore, is not to condone the use of nutritional supplements but instead to emphasize the need for sound nutrition in the form of a balanced meal. The rationale is threefold. First, where do you draw the line on what is safe, ethically acceptable, and actually effective? Drawing the line on what and how much of a supplement to take is not always clear. For example, we can see little harm in taking megadoses of vitamin C, purportedly noted to ward off any chance of illness, such as the common cold. But, what about megadoses of creatine—a nutritional supplement that occurs naturally in red meat that reportedly helps in the training of "power" athletes? Or, what about taking a dose of a naturally occurring hormone in the body to gain more strength, such as HGH, or human growth hormone? Are all supplements safe? Supplements can contain banned substances because their labeling is unregulated (athletes who test positive for banned substances are disqualified from competition). A study by the International Olympic Committee determined that nearly 15 percent of 634 nutritional supplements contained prohibited substances. Certainly from a health point of view, it is at least important to know what one is truly ingesting.

Second, you should be seeking to gain an advantage by simply participating in good, old, hard judo training. This way of thinking is especially important to instill in younger judoka who should be taught to earn their success. Supplements mislead people to think that they are consuming a magical pill that will instantly produce results. In reality, there are no such shortcuts.

Third, you can neglect taking care of basic nutritional needs if you overlook the practice of eating a balanced meal. This can occur if you intentionally or unintentionally substitute certain food groups with supplements. For example, some judoka who consume powdered protein will begin to neglect getting their protein needs from eating meat. What occurs is the elimination of other benefits of meat such as vitamins, iron, and so on.

As we have seen in this chapter, sound nutritional habits are important for everyone whether one is a recreational or elite judoka. The overall point is that you should not replace a balanced meal and eating whole foods with supplements or artificial foods. Become informed about sound nutritional choices so that you can perform to your fullest.

Match Plans, Competitive Strategies, and Tactics

Strategies and tactics are important to judo because they are compatible with Professor Kano's premise that physical prowess is not always decisive. Judo is well suited to the implementation of strategy and tactics because the dynamic nature of judo allows for psychological and physical factors to be manipulated. Professor Kano never disputed the use of strength in judo but rather the unnecessary expenditure of it. With this in mind, and with the evolution of judo as an Olympic sport, competitive judoka must train many physical and mental components to become elite fighters.

The classical strategist in judo attempts to avoid a head-to-head confrontation. A sumo-type showdown has been frowned upon because the overt display of brute strength and force is incompatible with judo's definition—the yielding way. Judo can be decided with the first good throw, and matches can theoretically end in seconds. Many good fighters attack immediately and use a high-intensity and aggressive strategy. One of the fastest ippons on record was scored by Japan's Akio Kaminaga who threw his Philippine opponent in four seconds at the Tokyo Olympics in the open weight class. Likely the quickest match ever could be a three-second ippon recorded at the Barcelona Olympics in the 86-kilogram (190-pound) men's division where Andres Franco (Cuba) used morote-gari over his opponent from Zaire.

IPPON JUDO

Ippon judo, in which the ultimate aim is to score ippon, leads to exciting matches and should remain your overall match strategy. The preciseness and uncertainty of judo allows ippon to be attained virtually any time during the match. From a strategical perspective, ippon judo makes good sense. If you can finish the match as early as possible, you can conserve energy and decrease fatigue over the course of the tournament day, where it may take four to six matches to reach the medal round. It is important to give yourself the best recovery between matches where you can be up again any time after the minimum 10 minutes of rest. In addition, the less time you spend on the mat, the less opportunity your opponents have to scout out what techniques you have used. Ippon judo boosts your confidence, and your performance likely will enhance future matches.

Competitors at the elite level are serious, well conditioned, and trained to meet the demands of matches. Because of this and their all-important desire to win the match, judoka holding on to a lead often do not attempt ippon judo because it may involve risk of a win. Such strategies have hampered the action that judo potentially possesses (yet, the educated public can appreciate a good "chess match" despite its lack of dynamism). An overly defensive attitude relegates the match to inaction, is contrary to ippon judo, and can easily be identified as "negative judo." Fortunately, the rules are designed to encourage and reward you for attempting ippon.

DEVELOPING YOUR STRATEGY AND TACTICS

What if you have superior strength over the opponent who may have better technical ability? Is it wrong to utilize strength to gain an advantage? After all, in competitive judo, the end result to win is paramount. Differences in technical ability and physical conditioning among fighters at the elite levels are often not substantial, which makes strategy and tactics all the more important. Competitive judo has evolved to where the judoka seeks any possible edge to be successful.

Strategy can be defined as the overall match plan or goal to be achieved. For example, it could be the judoka's objective to end up on the ground knowing one is stronger in ne-waza than in the standing position. Tactics would be the actual methods used to achieve that goal. The judoka in this case may decide to attack with tomoe-nage knowing that an unsuccessful attempt would enable an opportunity to go into ground fighting. Obviously, if the attempt is successful (throw is good) that result is desired. The least preferred outcome would be that the tomoe-nage is countered. The judoka would have to weigh the consequences of being countered to the preferred opportunity to go into ne-waza fighting.

It is important to acknowledge that strategy and tactics must be carefully crafted. What works for one judoka may not necessarily work for another. You must study strategy and tactics and be prepared to use them knowing that many require fundamental prerequisites such as good fitness and technical ability. As well, if strategy and tactics are to make or break a match result, it would follow that mental factors will play a significant part both from a defensive and offensive perspective.

A key consideration is to match the strategy and its tactics to suit your physical abilities. A strong flurry of attacks designed to overwhelm the opponent will not work if you are less powerful and technically inferior. If you are well conditioned, however, attempting to keep a high tempo throughout the match so that you can wear your opponent down before opening up with your tokui-waza, or favorite techniques, is a good idea.

Rather than arbitrarily choosing from the multitude of techniques, follow a systematic approach based upon two premises: First, you will not be able to learn all the techniques and their variations. Therefore, you will need to be selective in those that you decide to acquire. Second, you will not be able to perform all the techniques you have chosen to learn at the same level of expertise. Therefore, you must be selective in choosing what techniques you want to perfect. A number of strategic variables need to be considered to formulate a strategic base that will represent your personal judo style:

• Attack areas. You need to attack at the main corners of the opponent. For example, you may have developed an attack to the left and right leg of the opponent (leg sweeps or ashi-waza), but you also need to balance with throws so the opponent cannot focus on defending any one single area.

• Technique options before and after an attack. You need to increase the options that can be carried out after a specific attack. For example, if your favorite throw is seoi-nage, numerous combinations can be linked into seoi-nage (for example, okuri-ashi-barai → seoi-nage) and also from seoi-nage (for example, seoi-nage → ouchi-gari).

• Left versus right. You will normally have a dominant side and rely on that side for the majority of attacks. It is to your advantage if you can complement with opposite-side attacks. It should be noted, however, that it will be impossible to acquire perfect symmetry and expertise in both left- and right-side attacks. The time and effort that it takes to achieve a high level of expertise against a resisting opponent may well be better spent on other strategic variables. An adequate level of left and right balance should be acquired for competition but not necessarily the identical level of expertise to either side. Rather, for example, your right-sided osoto-gari might be complemented with a left-sided okuri-ashi-barai.

Phil Takahashi, who is right-handed, developed the ability to attack from both left and right sides. One of his best attacks was a left tai-otoshi.

• Train weaknesses. The basic philosophy is to exploit your strengths and hide your weaknesses. If you are strong in standing judo (versus ground fighting), then you should make every effort to stay in the standing position. Conversely, if you are weak on the ground, you should avoid poor throws that may result in going to the ground or defending so the opponent gains position on top. Interestingly, however, you do the opposite in training. That is, it is important for you to practice your weaknesses during training and to avoid practicing your strengths. Training your weaknesses allows for more complete overall development and is captured in the saying, "A chain is only as strong as its weakest link."

Following are several more important strategic variables:

• Priority selections. Some data exists on the frequency of techniques used in competition and which are more successful than others. If there is a high percentage of scoring from one technique, and next to nil from another, it makes sense that you consider data in the selection of what works at the competitive level. There's no sense in practicing a particular technique if it's not used or rarely seen in competition.

• Physical attributes. You must consider your own physical attributes and use them to your advantage. Physical components important in judo are strength, flexibility, aerobic conditioning, and height, to name a few. For example, a judoka who is tall can use reach and the leverage created in throws such as tai-otoshi and uchi-mata.

- Balanced attack and defense. Good judoka have strong attacks, but the best are also strong in defense. Low-scoring matches that are close indicate the need to have good defense to win matches. Good defense means strong stand-up judo and not overly defensive or negative judo.

- A favorite technique, or tokui-waza. Having a favorite technique that you can rely upon or be known for is like having a secret weapon. In the final of the All-Japan Championships, Yamashita fought highly respected Matsui who took Yamashita to the last 20 seconds without a score. Yamashita pulled out his famous uchi-mata (although he was ruled out-of-bounds) that was the determining factor in his fifth consecutive championship.

- Develop what comes naturally. If a technique comes naturally, you should continue to develop it. Many judoka have their own idiosyncrasies and are known for their individual styles, however unorthodox they may be. Techniques that come easily are usually perfected quicker. Conversely, if you are having difficulty implementing a certain technique or lack the confidence to perform it well, there may be no sense in pursuing that technique further.

MATCH STRATEGIES

You will face many opponents, and it could be said that each fight will be different from the last. Even matches against the same opponent will differ in some way. Some opponents may fight in predictable ways whereas others may use different styles or be unorthodox in their approach. You must adjust to these differences by maximizing your personal strategies to fit your overall match strategies. Many situations will arise during a match, and you must choose the appropriate tactics. Judokas who can make quick and wise decisions in the heat of the battle gain a significant advantage over their opponents.

Scouting and Analyzing the Opponent

Scouting, or knowing what your opponent can do, is an important ingredient of an overall match strategy. Scouting can be very basic, from watching your opponents from the stands during a tournament to analyzing videotape and keeping statistics on techniques used. The objective of scouting is to utilize gathered information for developing strategies and tactics and gaining an advantage over the opponent psychologically. Scouting allows you to assess the opponent's strengths and weaknesses, techniques used, and overall fighting style. Scouting is not a new concept. Sun Tzu, a famous Chinese strategist whose collection of works are documented in the book, *The Art of War*, written in 500 B.C., stated, "If ignorant of both the enemy and of yourself, you are certain in every battle to be in peril." (*The Art of War*. Sun Tzu. Translated by Samuel B. Griffith. 1971. Oxford University Press. London. Pg. 84).

Scouting methods can vary in complexity and sophistication. The benefits are numerous, and you should take responsibility for knowing your opponents. Scouting sheets that indicate basic technical data, frequency of attacks, and strengths and weaknesses can be tabulated on-site. More detailed scouting sheets can be developed through videotape analysis, and subsequent matches can be tabulated to determine if patterns exist. You can then formulate your strategies based upon the information gathered, taking into account your individual capabilities and limitations.

Personal Reflections on Strategy— Allyn Takahashi

When I was a teenager, I had the opportunity to represent Ontario at the Canadian Youth Championship held in Edmonton, Alberta, in 1972. I watched all of the other competitors and found that the favorite to win my division had a beautiful uchimata, which he used to throw every opponent for ippon. He was tall and had long legs, whereas my stance was squat and hunched over—basically a defensive posture. I was a perfect target for uchi-mata. We both made the finals, and during the pause before our match, I asked my coach what I could do against the uchi-mata. My coach said simply, "Just move your leg behind yourself, and then use it for a tai-otoshi." He showed me that basically I would let my opponent come in to do the uchi-mata with my leg as bait. At the last instant, I would move it out of the way, and when his leg missed mine, I would throw him with his own momentum. We practiced the uchi-mata-sukashi a few times out of sight in a hallway.

When the referee called, "Hajime!" we gripped each other. I felt his strength and confidence, and immediately, I felt him setting me up. By an instinctive reaction, my leg moved back just as his leg swept past. I had reacted before consciously knowing that the uchi-mata was coming. I gave a great kiai [power shout,] and tried to get my leg in front for the tai-otoshi. His uchi-mata was so fast and powerful that he had already thrown himself.

Fortunately for me, he had not known that I had studied him. I knew his technique and how he set up. He had not seen my coach and me practicing. I had put everything into moving my leg out of the way. Fortunately, I reacted properly on his first attempt. If his first motion was just a snap of the gi to test my reactions, and I moved my leg in reaction, he would have discovered my entire strategy.

I cannot recommend using a defensive strategy whereby you wait for your opponent to do what you expect him to do. Had my opponent known that I was studying him, he could have faked an uchi-mata, and instead done a tai-otoshi. I would have been caught standing on one leg. All uchi-mata experts know this effective combination.

I stole a gold medal that day from a superior judoka by careful observation. Simply knowing an opponent's tokui-waza, however, is not enough. Judoka do many subconscious actions before their technique. It is possible to read an opponent's moves. My father, Masao Takahashi, would get us to do randori blindfolded so that we would become sensitive to our opponents' kuzushi and setup techniques. At first it seems impossible, but there are many blind judoka and wrestlers as proof that it is possible to read an opponent.

Strategy of Attrition

The objective of the strategy of attrition is to wear down the opponent mentally or physically. This strategy works well in judo because you have the opportunity to manipulate the tempo and dictate the level of intensity in a match. You must be in good physical condition for attrition strategy to work. You must also use speed and movement to avoid potentially risky situations and to keep the opponent off-guard. For example, you should not attempt a poor seoi-nage attack that can be blocked and result in a defensive turtle position on the ground. Here, you will be unable to keep the tempo of the match high and even may find yourself in a position of vulnerability on the ground. A more favorable tactic would be to move quickly in kumi-kata and attack safely but repeatedly to tire the opponent down.

Attrition strategy applied at its best is classical warfare and relates well to judo. Its concept clearly shows how relentless attack and patience will eventually bring the opponent to a state of vulnerability. The opponent, once tired and unable to successfully finish attacks, becomes demoralized.

Phil Takahashi keeps his opponent off-guard with attacks. By putting the opponent in positions of vulnerability (off balance), one is able to maintain pressure and attack when match conditions are favorable.

Technical-Tactical Situations

Technical-tactical situations are instances during the match where you can apply a specific technique(s) given a specific situation. For example, if the opponent is pushing hard to force you to step backward and out-of-bounds at the edge of the mat, you can throw to go out-of-bounds (likely what the opponent may think you will do) but actually attack in the opposite direction using ouchi-gari, for example, to throw toward the center of the mat. In this case, you deceive the opponent by attacking into him.

Zone Tactics

The red danger zone that lines the perimeter of the competition area is one meter (a little more than three feet) wide. When you enter the danger zone you must be wary of your positioning because stepping out could warrant a penalty. Even attacking and purposely going out-of-bounds can be judged as going against the spirit of judo. Some say the rule is rooted from ancient times when the samurai in combat needed to stay in bounds or fall off a cliff where certain or near death would be the consequence (for example, retreating back and attempting tomoe-nage out-of-bounds will be called a penalty to the attacker).

Modern-day tactics are a far cry from the battlefields of the samurai. What is evident, however, is that considerable action takes place near and in the danger zone. An attack that starts in the zone but lands the opponent outside the contest area is good and warrants a positive score. An attack that results in either or both competitors going out-of-bounds results in no score and resumes in the middle of the mat. The relative safety of attacking near the edge of the mat makes zone tactics all-important.

When on Offense

When on offense the main objective is to get your opponent to step out-of-bounds, subjecting him or her to a penalty, or put the opponent in a vulnerable position where you can attack, either out-of-bounds or toward the center of the mat. In both cases, you have to use the zone to your advantage because you must make the opponent react differently because of it. The key in the first instance is to make the opponent lose his or her mat awareness by attacking and feinting, so that the opponent steps out-of-bounds inadvertently. In the second scenario, the opponent responds the opposite, that is, he or she is too preoccupied being near the edge of the mat and either cannot react in time for your attack or is unable to move appropriately to defend against it.

Generally, the opponent's back should be facing toward the out-of-bounds so that you, as the attacker, have position to stay inside. Therefore, it is important to position the opponent quickly and attempt to prevent him or her from coming back into the center or circling back in the center.

When on Defense

By virtue of being on defense you are at a disadvantage. If you are backed up in the zone you are not in a good position. It is best to get out of this situation with neutrality by going out-of-bounds and resuming the match in the middle standing. Be careful not to attack out of desperation because, if unsuccessful, your attack could be countered or put you in a vulnerable position. If you attack to go out-of-bounds there is a chance that it could be viewed negatively and subjected to a penalty. Consider the following options: (1) Let the opponent attack with the hopes it is not decisive and you both go out-of-bounds. The call would be to resume in the middle of the mat. (2) Attempt to circle or push forward to get out of the zone and obtain more space. (3) Be patient and wait it out with the hope the situation improves or you catch a mistake by the opponent. Remember, the opponent has an offensive mind-set and may overlook his or her own vulnerability or your capabilities to attack.

Maintaining the Lead

A number of factors become important when maintaining the lead. Almost always, you should avoid being behind in a match. That is, you should always attempt to lead the match and win it from the outset. The need to maintain a lead typically occurs near the end of the match when you are willing to ride the time out and settle for the win, whether it is by a small technical score such as koka or by protecting a larger score such as waza-ari. In either case, you must keep the following from occurring:

- Tiring out so your defense becomes vulnerable
- Looking too defensive so you get penalized for noncombativity or negative judo
- Losing focus so you are caught off-guard
- Putting yourself in a poor position where you are susceptible to being thrown or countered
- Making false attacks
- Making poor attempts at throws that can be countered

A common mistake when maintaining a lead is becoming too defensive or assuming a defensive mind-set. The opponent will take advantage of this by becoming the aggressor and starting to control the match. If the opponent senses any sign of weakness (defensive attitude), he or she will immediately capitalize on the opportunity.

To avoid appearing defensive, you must first not fight the clock. That is, you should avoid watching the clock expire. You must fight hard right through to the end without regard to time. Many examples of matches lost have occurred where judoka have attempted to hang on hoping time expires. Following are suggestions for maintaining your lead without looking defensive:

- Change styles and pace of the match. This will keep the opponent off-guard and will avoid making you look passive.
- Go for stoppages in the match. For example, you can attack near the edge of the mat to go out-of-bounds to resume in the center. This tactic can allow you to get out of a bad grip or situation. Going for stoppages also allows you to use time fighting for grip when resuming the match in the center.
- Go to the ground. If you are confident in ne-waza, going to the ground is a good tactic because ground fighting requires position, which can be thwarted easier than in standing situations. More time can be wasted fighting on the ground where there are more isometric situations. Choose a way to get to the ground that is safe and nonrisky. Making a false attack to get to the ground, for example, could net you a penalty.
- Focus on the fight for grip. Take your time and focus to get a grip to prevent a good attack from the opponent.
- Avoid risky positions. Stay clear from any position where the opponent can make an attack. For example, do not attack poorly, which can be countered.
- Stay calm. Many judoka panic when leading near the end of a match, feeling the pressure of the situation. It is possible the opponent can make mistakes that can lead to your counterattack. Remember, too, if you have the lead it usually means you are in control of the match. Many times, winning is only a matter of maintaining control and staying composed.

Fighting Against a Technically Better Opponent

There are two basic strategies to employ when you are fighting against a more technically proficient opponent: First, do not allow your opponent to employ his or her game plan or techniques. Do this by attacking first, trying to end the match early, and catching your opponent off-guard. Second, try to keep the match as close as possible and use attrition strategy.

Fighting a Stronger, Less Technical Opponent

Avoid situations where an opponent's superior strength and conditioning will take a toll on your performance. Attempt to finish the match quickly, or create opportunities where you can attack without putting yourself in vulnerable positions or situations.

Coming From Behind

Coming from behind requires a certain mind-set. You must truly believe you can do it. Usually, in this case the situation is complicated by time pressure. That is, you must obtain a score within a certain time left in the match. Being able to think clearly is important because the situation can change quickly as time runs out. For example, if 30 seconds are left in the match there is still enough time for you to get a grip and attack at least one or two times. If only 10 seconds are left in the match, however, the situation has changed dramatically. In this situation, you are under huge time pressure to do the same. Some attribute scoring ippon when coming from behind as luck or a bad break for the opponent. More often than not, however, coming from behind successfully is a result of two factors: First, you must believe a victory is truly possible. Second, you must make a quick assessment of the situation so that you can execute the proper technical and tactical response. It doesn't make sense, for example, to attack with koka techniques when ippon is needed.

A Basketball Example

An NBA basketball playoff game between the Los Angeles Lakers and the Denver Nuggets (May 2004) offers a good example of coming from behind. The Lakers managed to take the lead by scoring with 11 seconds left in the game to put them up by one point. The opposing Nuggets quickly rallied back, knowing the Lakers would go into a defensive mode. With only two seconds remaining the Nuggets scored, always knowing they could still score even with so little time remaining. But the Lakers called time-out, and the clock stopped at .4 seconds remaining in the game with a throw-in from the side. Yes, the Lakers made a dramatic come-from-behind play to win the game with the clock showing .4 seconds left. With only 11 seconds left in the game the lead changed three times. Ippon, too, can be scored with only seconds left in the match.

EVALUATING YOUR WINS AND LOSSES

Experience is said to be important in almost every endeavor, and certainly this is true in judo where learning is continual. It fits, therefore, that self-evaluation after every match is important, whether one wins or loses. It is said you can learn more by losing than by winning. This may be because winners tend to overlook evaluating the match with a critical eye. You must seek to improve regardless of the result because virtually every match is a unique experience that allows one to develop further.

Michael Jordan, who some consider to be the best basketball player of all time, said, "I've failed over and over again, that's why I succeed." The message in his quote clearly shows how losing has contributed to his success. It's okay to fail as long as you can learn from it. In Jordan's case, his failures may not be regarded as such by others, yet, his expectations of himself on a relative scale show that he was able to learn from his mistakes.

Be wary of dwelling excessively on your mistakes. This negative mind-set will only bring you down further and negatively affect your development. The saying, "there's no sense crying over spilled milk," fits the misdirected energy and focus you can preoccupy yourself with after a defeat. You especially want to avoid dwelling on losses during a tournament when you could instead be preparing yourself to win your next match.

Ray Takahashi learned a valuable lesson from losing the gold medal match at the Commonwealth Wrestling Championships. He lost to an opponent whom he had beaten two months earlier at the World Championships. Being overly confident, even a little cocky, his subpar performance was not enough on that day. The loss was a valuable learning experience for Takahashi, who subsequently never underestimated his opponents and avoided being overconfident in his attitude.

One way of better evaluating oneself is by becoming more knowledgeable. It is reasonable to think that the more educated you are about something, the more you can make an informed decision. You should therefore seek to become more educated about judo and all aspects that relate to it.

The following are some examples to broaden your knowledge of judo:

- Develop a library. Hold on to all books, magazines, videos, and other sources relating to judo.

- Watch to learn. You can learn a great deal by watching. There's a difference between watching for entertainment and watching to learn. Know the difference.

- Keep a logbook (or training diary) in which to document your training and other pertinent information. Keep it simple so you can make entries with as little as 5 to 10 minutes a day. This book can include useful information on your activities and serve as a motivator.

- Read the rules. Many judoka have never read the rules and learn only by experiencing. Reading the rules will deepen your comprehension.

- Learn from other sports. You should attempt to appreciate other sports and know more about what good things (and bad things) they can provide in terms of perspective. For example, the sport of golf is excellent for learning about composure. After missing a putt, the golfer must perform again immediately and not let a previous setback affect her next swing.

- Be a student. To be a student means that you are willing to learn. Very few persons, if any, get to a level where they have acquired all knowledge. Be receptive to learning and be better because of it.

UNCERTAINTY OF SPORT

Part of sport is its uncertainty, which allows for upsets and unpredictable outcomes despite all the proper training and preparation. It could be said that it is impossible to know everything that could happen during competition. The term "experience" is used to explain how you can become wiser so you are better prepared to deal with competitive nuances. And it is true that years of training and competing add up to make you better prepared. But, some things just happen and are out of our control despite our best efforts to prepare well.

Consider some real-life occurrences:

- A competitor does not make weight.
- A competitor gets injured and cannot perform optimally.
- A competitor misses the match.
- The referee gives a bad call that affects the outcome of the match.

A Japanese phrase captures this phenomenon—"Shikata ga nai." It means, "it can't be helped" or "no help for it." Sometimes things just happen for no reason. Some call it fate; others call it luck. Whatever it is called, you must know that some things are out of your control and that uncertainty in sport does happen. This does not mean you use such uncertainty as a way out or to make excuses if a negative outcome occurs. Rather, sometimes you must simply acknowledge that shikata gai nai: Uncertainty occurs, know when it happens, accept it, and deal with the consequences.

An example of uncertainty of sport happened to Phil Takahashi. He had a grueling match as he advanced toward the medal round at the 1981 World Championships. In his upcoming match against Pavel Petrikov of Czechoslovakia in the 60-kilogram (132 pound) weight class, he had no time to recover. A win would put him in the final, but he was physically exhausted and his arms were aching with lactic acid. He recalls: "I didn't have enough time to get my arms back, and I recall seeing the clock count down five minutes [a match length was used as the maximum recovery time]. I lost a close one, and I really believe if I was fully recovered it could have been a different outcome." Takahashi ended up with the bronze, and Petrikov settled with silver after losing to Yasuhiko Moriwaki of Japan in the final.

TIPS TO CONSIDER DURING COMPETITION

- Arrive at the competition site early. Be familiar with the surroundings and get on the competition mats to warm up if possible.

- Have a good idea when you are going to compete. This knowledge will dictate when to warm up and whether you have time for a snack or drink.

- Warm up properly. A proper warm-up is critical for the first match of the day (usually first matches are the most difficult to prepare for and most upsets happen in first matches).

- Cool down after a match. Recovery is very important and a light cool-down actually can aid in ridding the body of lactic acid from the muscles (the burning, tired feeling that occurs after intense activity, for example, in the arms after extensive gripping).

- Rest between matches. Find a comfortable place to sit and scout opponents. Don't waste energy standing, and don't warm up for the next match too early (or too late).

- Eat and drink (if timing permits) immediately after a match. Liquid is easier to digest than food.

- Accept the fact that nervousness is normal (and remember that everyone else is nervous too).

Remember, as you progress in your practice, you are faced with many strategic and tactical decisions due to the dynamic nature of the sport, which involves a high number of technical and physical components. This dynamism adds to the flare of judo because no single factor makes for a successful performance. The dynamic movement in a match and the opportunity to use strategic elements such as time, space, and force, make matches extremely challenging. Success in judo is not relegated only to the most fit, the strongest, or even the most technically proficient. Winning matches often go to judoka who are able to apply their strategies and tactics better than their opponent. Remember, it is not always the best judoka who wins but rather those who are the best prepared.

Self-Defense
Applications

One of the main reasons people take up judo is to learn self-defense. Although self-defense is not the main thrust of judo teaching, judo is undoubtedly effective in this area. Judo teaches many self-defense techniques including the use of weapons. Such techniques, however, are only practiced in kata because of the risk of injury. As well, rules in sport judo restrict many techniques and situations that can be performed because the emphasis and specialty is on throwing and ground techniques.

In many ways, the focus and teaching of judo as sport has de-emphasized the study of judo for self-defense, and critics even question its credibility as an effective method. Judo discourages confrontation; recall that the translation of judo is the gentle or yielding way. As such, the teachings of judo discourage its use outside the dojo; doing so is thought to lead to misuse and misdirection of judo's true meaning.

People tend to compare martial arts against one another to find out which is better for self-defense studies. These individuals often want to hear a simple answer such as, "Judo is best because you can throw and armlock your opponent," or "Karate is the best because you can kick them before they know what's happening." But the real answer is not that simple. Clearly, throwing and grappling is judo's specialty, so if one wants to be proficient in throwing, judo would be best. Similarly, if one wants to specialize in kicking, a martial art such as taekwondo or karate would be good. Masao Takahashi explains it this way: "If you have to compare martial arts, then compare them as a mountain to a river. The mountain should not look down on the river because it's lowly, and the river should not make fun of the mountain because it can't dance and move." Martial arts should be compared in terms of what they do offer instead of in terms of what they do not. One should also avoid comparing martial arts to one another, which is like comparing apples and oranges.

Some dojos or their senseis base their reputations and form their philosophies around the question of martial arts' effectiveness for self-defense, and some do little service to the martial arts by doing so. If true Kodokan judo is to be taught, a sensei would be reluctant to even attempt to answer the question. To answer it would be to follow the bait of diverging away from the true objectives of judo. Answering it could not be accomplished without an informed and in-depth response, something that the questioner is not looking for.

The prevalence of mixed martial arts (MMA) contests, which have appeal to many for their broad range of one-on-one combat styles, is regarded as the ultimate test of the effectiveness of the martial arts. MMA is growing rapidly, and at its inception few rules were put in place and fighters fought until one person was subdued or knocked out. Many MMA fighters have a base martial arts or combative background from which they developed, although the increasing popularity and growth of MMA has now established it as a fighting system in its own right. Brazilian-style jujitsu has gained much attention as a method of combat in MMA contests primarily because of its emphasis on ground fighting. This fighting style utilizes many of the same principles of throwing and ground fighting as judo.

The MMA event, which became popular in the 1990s, is now a full-fledged sporting event that has expanded and developed to produce specialized athletes. As MMA evolves further, so too will the rules to prevent serious injury to the fighters and to keep the event attractive in the eyes of the spectator. Changes to rules have been quick in the short history of MMA to limit ground fighting, which is considered boring to the uneducated spectator. Implementing rounds so that long, continuous ground fighting is broken to resume a standing position is now common. Competitors are also stood up when inactivity or a perceived stalemate occurs on the ground (like in judo). It will be interesting to see how MMA rules further evolve as the sport itself evolves. Already, since its recent inception, numerous rules have been implemented to ensure the safety of the participants and to make it appealing to the spectator, similar to challenges faced in judo.

Judoka are discouraged from engaging in MMA as it goes against the philosophy of judo. As a judoka, one is expected to stay within the bounds of judo training and test oneself within the sport of judo. By and large, this maxim has been followed, with few judoka going against the norm.

Credibility of Judo

One of the first fighters to go against the norm of practicing judo inside the dojo was Masahiko Kimura, who turned professional in 1950 and is reported to have beaten Helio Gracie, a Brazilian jujitsu champion for 20 years. In a well-publicized match that contested judo against jujitsu, Kimura broke Gracie's arm with ude-garami, although Gracie never gave up, he was clearly beaten.

JUDO PHILOSOPHY IN SELF-DEFENSE

Judo is not simply a system of learning techniques for self-defense, although learning self-defense can be a reason for taking it up. In some ways, judoka could be said to have learned a greater form of self-defense by avoiding and walking away from confrontation. The underlying objective of judo, as created by Professor Kano, is to create people that are humble, helpful, kind, and calm. People with self-confidence do not need to prove themselves by fighting simply to preserve honor.

Judo training is a great form of self-defense because of its physicality and the contact that gives one a sense of control and resistance. Randori provides a realistic setting where one fights for grip, and attack and defense are tested. Judo specializes in throwing so judoka are trained in gripping, which develops hand speed and the ability to control the opponent. Training with various partners allows one to appreciate differences and tests one's strengths and weaknesses. Confidence will emerge in judo study, and for some, an increased sense of self-esteem.

Although judo can serve as a form of self-defense, it is important to understand its limitations. Judo as a form of self-defense is not all encompassing (no martial art is), and you must always be wary of entering into self-defense confrontations (ambush attacks, being outnumbered, and concealed weapons) where there are few rules in place to limit a multitude of unexpected situations for which one may not be trained.

A judoka that only concentrates on the sport or competitive side of judo may not be prepared to defend weapons or striking attacks. There are self-defense moves against armed and unarmed attackers, but the judoka must train diligently for these situations. Conversely, a judoka can often restrain someone without having to strike or hurt him or her.

Basic Strategy

The basic strategy when faced with a self-defense situation is to perform what you are best trained to do and what suits you best from an individual perspective. Generally, you can apply the strategy of getting close enough to grip the assailant to apply a throw. This strategy has to be applied quickly to avoid strikes. Once on the ground, you can subdue the opponent with a hold, choke, or armlock. For example, let's say an assailant pushes you in the chest. Because you are trained to fight for grip, you should grip the assailant's jacket after being pushed as soon as possible. Retaliating by pushing back is not preferred since it may provoke an attack from the outside. A grip on the assailant will give you control. The type of technique to apply will depend largely on what you feel most comfortable attacking with.

Police Tactics: Without Strikes, With Strikes

Judo suits the self-defense needs of police officers because the emphasis is on control rather than striking. In many police confrontations, strikes are not desired partly because of the extreme consequences strikes produce. For example, a strike can cut or even break bones and, targeted to the head, can result in a concussion. Many times, police situations require the ability to control and subdue the assailant while leaving no visible marks. Avoiding strikes also removes any suspicion of excessive police force from public scrutiny.

The throwing specialty of judo is valuable in taking the assailant down, and the holding and submission techniques are ideal when the fight goes to the ground. Throws such as osoto-gari and tai-otoshi are good choices because they can be executed fast and from a quick and secure grip. Judo would be suitable for police or any other persons where the potential for physical confrontation may occur (for example, hospital workers, probation officers, security personnel, and prison guards).

Judo for Police Officers

In 1932 the Royal Canadian Mounted Police accepted judo over boxing and wrestling as the form of combat to teach its police officers. This marked the first time in Canada that Caucasians received instruction in judo. When King George VI made a visit to Canada in 1939, the RCMP and 13 black-belt judoka acted as bodyguards.

Following are some ways that judo techniques can be applied in various self-defense situations.

From Lunge to Harai-Goshi

A judoka's hands are fast. Many people underestimate the speed with which judoka can catch and block, developed through grip fighting in randori and tournaments. This speed is advantageous in situations where the initial confrontation is jostling and pushing. Judoka are accustomed to gripping quickly, whether it's an assailant's jacket or bare arm. Still, you need to be wary of the possibility that an assailant will attack first with strikes.

The attacker lunges from a sideways angle into the defender.

The defender deflects arms by taking the inside, reaching behind the attacker's head with the right arm and trapping with the left arm.

As the attacker moves forward, the defender pulls the attacker into position and, sweeping hard with the right leg, throws with harai-goshi.

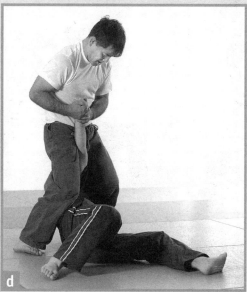

As the attacker is thrown, the defender hangs on to the attacker's right arm while keeping balance in the standing position. The defender steps over the attacker's head with his left leg and squeezes the knees together to apply juji-gatame to the attacker's arm.

Against Right-Handed Slap (Strike) to Osoto-Gari

Note the importance of body turning or zoning out of the line of attack. Zoning out or getting away from the direct attack is vital in most self-defense techniques.

The attacker attempts to slap (strike) with his right hand.

Reverse angle of attacker striking defender, and defender blocking by moving and slapping the attacker's arm down and across the body.

The defender pivots on the left leg while pushing down and controlling the attacker's arm.

The defender pivots on her left foot and starts sweeping into osoto-gari and pushing with the right hand against the attacker's shoulder.

The defender follows through with the sweep, throwing the attacker to the ground.

The defender can strike the attacker's head area to finish the situation.

Push to Waki-Gatame

Waki-gatame, armpit armlock, is an effective armlock which is very simple to apply either standing, sitting, or on the ground. The arm must be kept extended and held tightly under the armpit.

The attacker pushes in while reaching with his left arm. Defender reaches with her left arm and grabs the attacker's wrist.

The defender pivots to turn into arm, pulling it to keep it extended. The defender traps attacker's arm under her right armpit so pressure can be exerted from above.

The defender keeps the attacker's arm straight and drives her body weight on his arm to force him to the ground

The defender pressures down with her right armpit and pries the attacker's arm in waki-gatame.

Against Two-Handed Push to Tomoe-Nage

The defender should make sure he or she has a strong grip on the attacker's arm. The defender maintains his or her pull while pushing hard with his or her foot low on the attacker's abdomen.

a

The defender yields backward when the attacker pushes forward.

b

The defender grabs the attacker's arms and places one foot on the attacker's lower abdomen while sitting down close to the heel of his other foot. The defender's kicking leg should be kept bent, especially at the beginning of the throw to let the defender get in close and so power can be generated by extending the leg to throw the attacker over.

c

The defender rolls with the momentum in a back-roll action with the attacker as he is thrown over.

d

The defender completes the tomoe-nage by rolling through on top of the attacker and he can strike if desired.

Against Headlock to Ura-Nage

This is a very common counter seen in judo competition. The fall can be very dangerous to the attacker's head and neck even on good mats so a crash mat may be more safe.

a

The attacker has a headlock around the defender.

b

The defender clinches around the attacker's waist and moves around sideways and brings his feet in close and perpendicular to the attacker's. The defender stays low, keeping the neck tense.

c

The defender uses his legs to lift the attacker up by propping with the hips, keeping a tight clinch. The defender can arch back to generate more power and follow through in the throw.

d

The defender turns as he throws the attacker over with ura-nage. The defender turns to land on top of the attacker to go into ground fighting.

Against Neck Grab

The very popular ouchi-gari is used in this sequence. Care should be taken not to slap the attacker's ears too hard as damage to the ear drums could occur. The hooking foot should be close to the ground to prevent the attacker's countering.

a

The attacker reaches for a choke with both hands around the defender's neck.

b

The defender lowers her body and shoots her arms inside the attacker's arms in an upward direction.

c

The defender reaches up and spreads the arms to break choke.

d

The defender quickly slaps the attacker's ears.

e

The defender attacks with ouchi-gari to throw attacker backward.

f

The defender follows through with a strike to the attacker's groin.

Against Clinch to Hadaka-Jime

The defender withdraws the legs, lowers the hips, and easily performs a knee strike on the attacker. The leg grab is another common attack. The defender should be careful whenever applying techniques involving the neck.

a

The defender is wary of an attack by the attacker from the outside.

b

As the attacker attacks the defender's lower body, the defender moves his legs back while reaching over the attacker's head to apply hadaka-jime with the right arm, ensuring that the radius bone (near thumb) goes across the attacker's throat.

c

The defender applies the choke while kneeing the attacker with the right leg.

d

The defender applies the choke with more force by lifting the attacker up by pushing forward with his body and lifting the arms.

Against Strike to Hiza-Guruma

The defender steps away (to the right) and catches the attacker's arm. At the same time, the defender uses his or her force and wheels the attacker around while blocking his or her knee.

a

The defender anticipates a right-handed strike from the attacker.

b

The defender blocks the strike with the left hand from the inside and traps the attacker's arm above the elbow.

c

The defender pulls with the left arm forward while blocking with his left leg against the attacker's right leg.

d

The defender pulls hard while turning so the attacker gets thrown forward over the blocked leg (hiza-guruma).

e

The defender follows though with hiza-guruma, keeping his balance.

f

The defender can finish with a punch to the attacker's face area.

Against Kick to Ouchi-Gari

Here is a situation where the defender moves in toward the attacker, blocking his or her kicking leg, scooping in and reaping the attacker's support leg. Care must be taken when throwing by gripping the attacker to prevent dropping the attacker on his or her head or neck in practice.

a

The defender shields his body with the left arm as the attacker kicks. The defender's right hand is up and ready to strike if needed.

b

The defender blocks the kick and grabs the attacker's leg while moving into the attacker.

c

The defender lifts the attacker's leg and sweeps the attacker's support leg with his right leg with ouchi-gari.

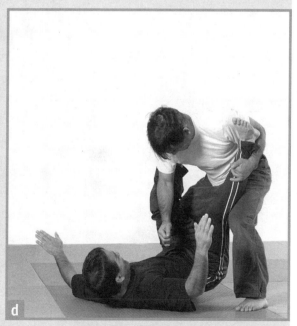

d

The defender follows through and can finish with a punch to the attacker's groin.

Takedowns

Takedowns by attacking the legs are often associated with wrestling (Olympic Freestyle), which specializes in taking an opponent to the ground. Judo incorporates leg attacks, but they are not as specialized as in wrestling because rules prohibit prolonged hanging on to the leg(s) with the hands. Despite this rule, the use of the hands to grab the legs to throw or take the opponent down in judo is now used more frequently and is also commonplace in tournaments (for example, kuchiki-taoshi, kata-guruma variations). Leg attacks are a better choice than throws in some cases. A poor attempt at a throw could result in turning your back to the assailant, putting you in a bad position.

As a self-defense application, takedowns certainly have their place in off-the-mat situations. Part of the reason for their effectiveness is the unusualness of a leg attack. People are not familiar with being attacked at the legs and hence are not familiar with how to mount a defense. In the sport of wrestling, wrestlers specialize in takedowns so their stances are low to protect these types of attacks. In a typical confrontation, however, a person usually engages with the upper body with a push or strike. A quick attack to the legs is an effective method to take your opponent down, especially if the attack catches the opponent off-guard.

Morote-Gari: Double-Leg Takedown

The defender drops his or her head to evade the attacker's arm, driving his or her shoulder into the attacker's chest. The defender immediately reaches behind the attacker's knees with both hands and, reaping both of the attacker's legs, throws him or her back.

a

The attacker pushes the defender with right hand.

b

The defender deflects arm up with the left arm while lowering head and stepping in with the right foot.

c

The defender drives forward, hitting the attacker in the ribs with the right shoulder while reaching behind the attacker's knees and driving the attacker backwards by stepping in with his right leg to throw him on his back.

d

The defender strikes the attacker while he is on his back.

Ground Attacks and Escapes

Getting into a strong (strategic) position where you can submit and control your opponent is extremely important in modern judo, mixed martial arts, and self-defense. It is important not to let your opponent get behind you where you have little offensive opportunities. Many judoka and wrestlers make this mistake, competing under the competition-rule mentality. Being able to get control of your opponent's body by holds is important and can tire out your opponent and make submissions easily attainable.

Freeing Leg From Side to Kesa-Gatame

When your opponent controls your leg, he or she nullifies your advantage. Keep your balance on top and use your free leg to help free your trapped leg.

The defender is on top of the attacker's right side with attacker scissoring defender's right leg.

The defender pushes with the left foot against the attacker's scissored legs.

The defender slips his leg out and secures for kesa-gatame.

The defender turns slightly to slip his right knee out while pushing with his left foot against the attacker's top (left) leg scissors.

Freeing Leg From Side to Ushiro-Kesa-Gatame

Freeing the legs on the ground takes time but is important for maintaining control of your opponent. It is very subtle and not really visible but very important in ground fighting.

The defender's right leg is trapped in attacker's scissors. The defender has a half-mount position on top of the attacker and maintains control with the left hand on the attacker's lapel.

The defender shifts his body to the attacker's right side and pushes with his right hand against the attacker's left leg to loosen scissors. The defender can use left leg (knee) to help push the attacker's right scissored leg down.

The defender wiggles his right leg to slip his knee out while pushing with the right arm against the attacker's left leg.

The defender slips right leg out and holds the attacker in ushiro-kesa-gatame.

Belt Lift

This technique demonstrates another situation where you lift your opponent's legs up to bypass the legs.

The defender is in-between the attacker's legs and grips underneath the attacker to grab his belt.

The defender stands and lifts the attacker, clearing the guard.

The defender controls the attacker by holding his belt with the right hand and using the right knee over the attacker's left arm to prevent turning. The defender grips the attacker's pant legs tightly at the knees and drives his knuckles downwards, keeping his knees together. The defender passes the legs while pushing the knees away.

The defender presses down and secures yoko-shiho-gatame.

Roll Over With Space

The use of the legs in groundwork is very important. The legs, if used properly, can be like two extra arms. The legs can change an advantage situation for your opponent to a situation where you have control.

The defender is on his back in the guard position. The defender utilizes the space between him and the attacker by positioning his body so that the arms and legs can be used to turn the attacker over.

As the defender's right leg lifts and kicks the attacker's inner thigh, the defender's right arm pushes and the left arm pulls. The defender's left leg can block or hook over the attacker's right leg.

Leg Hike

It is important not to be caught in a situation where your opponent can use his or her legs. Bypassing the legs is vital in groundwork.

The defender steps up with the right leg and reaches under the attacker's left leg behind the knees.

The defender lifts the leg up and across the body to clear the guard. While clearing the leg, the defender grips the attacker's lapel to control the attacker from turning away once the leg is hiked.

The defender secures by pressing down into yoko-shiho-gatame. When hiking the leg over it is important that the defender keeps the opposite arm short and close to the body for the attacker's counter with sankaku-jime.

Tsukkomi-Jime Counter to Waki-Gatame

This is a common situation whenever your opponent straightens his or her arm to resist or choke you. You use that energy and apply an armlock.

The defender can counter with waki-gatame when the attacker's arm is extended and pushing with the choke, tsukkomi-jime.

The defender grabs the attacker's wrist to keep the attacker's arm secure while turning into the armlock. The defender's armpit contacts the attacker at or above the elbow.

Turn to Guard

It is important not to let your opponent get behind you. This can be a bad habit of many judoka who stall or wait for a referee to break the match from long ground-work. It is vital always to face your opponent. This is a useful technique to position yourself to face your opponent when he or she is behind you.

Turn to guard. The defender is underneath and attempts to get out so as not to give his back to the attacker.

The defender posts with the right hand and sits the right leg across to turn his body towards the attacker.

The defender continues turning to face in the guard position by keeping the left leg bent so it can come across the attacker's body.

Juji-Gatame Roll From Top

The cross armlock, juji-gatame, is a very strong finishing technique on the ground and many variations are used. Neil Adams of Great Britain, world champion and Olympic gold medalist, and Peter Seisenbacher of Austria both used this technique.

The defender's right leg is trapped in the attacker's scissors. The defender has a half-mount position on top of the attacker.

The defender shifts his body to the attacker's right side and pushes with the right hand against the attacker's left leg to loosen scissors. The defender can use the left leg (knee) to help push the attacker's right scissored leg down.

The defender wiggles the right leg to slip the knee out while pushing with the right arm against the attacker's left leg.

Reverse angle: The defender continues to roll and sits up to secure arm and establish a perpendicular position to that of the attacker. The defender slips the right leg out and holds attacker in ushiro-kesa-gatame.

Sankaku-Jime: Triangular Lock

A triangular choke is done in many situations from different angles, as shown below. An alternate version, with the defender beginning the lock on the back is detailed in photos a and b on the top of page 191.

Sankaku-jime from front. The defender squats over the top of the attacker from the front and uses the left arm to catch the attacker's right arm. The defender inserts right heel behind the attacker's left arm.

The defender pulls sideways to turn the attacker to his back. While falling, the defender keeps the attacker's right arm trapped by gripping his own lapel with the left hand. The defender's left leg wraps around the attacker's head while the defender's right leg inserts deep to trap the attacker's left arm.

The defender adjusts his position sideways and grabs the attacker's left arm, pulling it tight against the attacker's head.

The defender locks legs together and inserts the left foot behind the right to choke with sankaku-jime, or uses the left hand to push the attacker's arm away to armlock.

In an alternative version of the triangular lock, the defender is on his back in the guard position. As the attacker attempts to clear the defender's right leg by scooping underneath with the left arm, the defender slides up.

The defender's right leg goes behind his left knee. The defender extends and pushes the attacker's trapped right arm across his body while the defender squeezes with his legs.

Jigoku-Jime Combination

This technique uses a very quick and strong choke entry and finishes with a combination into an armlock and a hold and back to armlock.

a

The defender inserts the left choking hand by grabbing the attacker's right lapel. The defender steps high and over the attacker while grabbing the attacker's lower-right pant leg.

b

The defender keeps grips and rolls the attacker over.

c

The defender rolls the attacker so he lands on his back while the defender maintains a grip on his leg and choking hand.

d

The defender pulls with the left choking hand and adjusts body position sideways.

The defender has the option of switching to armlock (juji-gatame). The defender lets go of the attacker's left arm and catches his right arm.

The defender steps over the attacker's head with the left leg to enter juji-gatame. The defender straightens the attacker's right arm to make the armlock effective by pushing down with the legs.

The defender has the option of switching to hold. The defender uses right hand to pull own lapel to left hand.

The defender keeps the left hand on own lapel to secure the attacker's right hand and to revert back to the armlock option if desired. The defender's right hand grips the attacker's pant leg while the defender's left leg moves back for balance.

It's important to keep in perspective that judo is not just self-defense—it is much more than that. After reading the chapters on the evolution and philosophy of judo and its dual role as art and sport, you can surmise that the teaching of self-defense is only one aspect of judo's original purpose. Professor Kano believed that as one masters the skills and techniques of judo, one also develops fully as a person. Ironically, this further development lessens the need for and the role of self-defense as one develops more competence with training and avoids situations where conflict can develop.

Aim always to practice the principles of maximum efficiency and mutual welfare and benefit—the guiding mottos of judo. Through judo practice, such as in randori, you develop not only the skills of attack and defense but also the ability to react to situations in daily life with the maximum use of your mind and body. As such, you are able to apply the principles of judo from an individual perspective and to ultimately become a better contributing person within society as a whole. As Professor Kano stated, "Make best use of your energies, and go forward together with your opponent."

APPENDIX

A LISTING OF NAGE-WAZA AND KATAME-WAZA

The gokyo, or gokyo no waza, is a set of 40 throws that represent the standard throwing techniques in judo. Originally, Professor Kano established 40 throws in 1886 and they are depicted in the nage no kata (see chapter 4). An additional 17 throws were added in 1920. In 1986 shimeisho no waza, or supplementary techniques, were officially recognized.

Advancing in judo requires knowledge and the ability to demonstrate the throws of the gokyo and shimeisho no waza. Judoka are expected to know more techniques as they progress in rank and are tested on their knowledge and ability to demonstrate the techniques. Judoka are graded in their Kyu grades (colored belts) within the dojo by their sensei while black-belt Dan grades are usually standardized within a country's judo federation.

The Kodokan upholds a standard for grading that regulates universal recognition of grading in black-belt Dan ranks. This has served judo well as it avoids variances in grading within organizations and countries that have shown to be problematic within other martial arts. A judoka who has attained black-belt status within one's country may choose to have his or her Dan rank registered with the Kodokan indicating that certification.

The technique listing in this appendix shows the recognized throwing and grappling techniques and their classification (first by their Japanese name, next by the English translation, and finally, by abbreviation code). Judoka should familiarize themselves with the names of the various throws and how they are classified as they progress.

TE-WAZA: HAND TECHNIQUES

Tai-otoshi
Body drop
TOS

Seoi-nage
Shoulder throw
SON

Kata-guruma
Shoulder wheel
KGU

Uki-otoshi
Floating drop
UOT

Sumi-otoshi
Corner drop
SOT

Sukui-nage
Scooping throw
SUK

Obi-otoshi
Belt drop
OOS

Seoi-otoshi
Shoulder drop
SOO

Yama-arashi
Mountain storm throw
YAS

TE-WAZA: HAND TECHNIQUES *(continued)*

Morote-gari
Two-hands reap
MGA

Kuchiki-taoshi
One-hand drop
KTA

Kibisu-gaeshi
Heel trip
KIG

Uchi-mata-sukashi
Inner-thigh reaping throw slip
UMS

Ippon-seoi-nage
One-armed shoulder throw
ISN

KOSHI-WAZA: HIP TECHNIQUES

Uki-goshi
Floating hip throw
UGO

Harai-goshi
Hip sweep
HRG

Tsurikomi-goshi
Lift-pull hip throw
TKG

Hane-goshi
Hip spring
HNG

O-goshi
Large hip throw
OGO

Ushiro-goshi
Back hip throw
USH

Utsuri-goshi
Hip transfer
UTS

Tsuri-goshi
Lifting hip throw
TGO

Koshi-guruma
Hip wheel
KOG

Daki-age
High Lift
STG

Sode-tsurikomi-goshi
Sleeve lift-pull hip throw
STO

ASHI-WAZA: LEG TECHNIQUES

Deashi-barai
Forward foot sweep
DAB

Hiza-guruma
Knee wheel
HIZ

Sasae-tsurikomi-ashi
Supporting foot lift-pull throw
STA

Osoto-gari
Large outer reap
OSG

Ouchi-gari
Large inner reap
OUG

Kosoto-gari
Small outer reap
KSG

Kouchi-gari
Small inner reap
KUG

Okuri-ashi-harai
Sweeping ankle foot sweep
OAB

Uchi-mata
Inner-thigh reaping throw
UMA

Kosoto-gake
Small outer hook
KSK

Ashi-guruma
Leg wheel
AGU

Harai-tsurikomi-ashi
Lift-pull foot sweep
HTA

(continued)

ASHI-WAZA: LEG TECHNIQUES *(continued)*

O-guruma
Large wheel
OGU

Osoto-guruma
Large outer wheel
OGR

Osoto-otoshi
Large outer drop
OSO

Tsubame-gaeshi
Swallow counter
TSU

Osoto-gaeshi
Large outer reaping throw
counter
OGA

Ouchi-gaeshi
Large inner reaping throw
counter
OUG

Kouchi-gaeshi
Small inner reaping throw
counter
KOU

Hane-goshi-gaeshi
Hip spring counter
HGG

Harai-goshi-gaeshi
Hip sweep counter
HGE

Uchi-mata-gaeshi
Inner-thigh reaping throw
counter
UMG

MA-SUTEMI-WAZA: FORWARD AND REAR SACRIFICE TECHNIQUES

Tomoe-nage
Circular throw
TNG

Sumi-gaeshi
Corner throw
SUG

Ura-nage
Back throw
UNA

Hikkomi-gaeshi
Pulling-down sacrifice throw
HKG

Tawara-gaeshi
Bag of rice throw
TWG

Obi-tori-gaeshi
Belt-grab throw
OTG

YOKO-SUTEMI-WAZA: SIDE SACRIFICE TECHNIQUES

Uki-waza
Floating throw
UWA

Yoko-gake
Side body drop
YGA

Yoko-guruma
Side wheel
YGU

Tani-otoshi
Valley drop
TNO

Yoko-wakare
Side separation
YWA

Yoko-otoshi
Side drop
YOT

Hane-makikomi
Springing wraparound throw
HNM

Uchi-mata-makikomi
Inner-thigh wraparound throw
UMM

Osoto-makikomi
Large outside wraparound throw
OSM

YOKO-SUTEMI-WAZA: SIDE SACRIFICE TECHNIQUES *(continued)*

Soto-makikomi
Outer wraparound throw
SMK

Uchi-makikomi
Inner wraparound throw
UMK

Harai-makikomi
Hip sweep wraparound throw
HRM

Daki-wakare
Rear trunk turnover
DWK

Kani-basami
Scissors throw
KBA

Kawazu-gake
Single leg entanglement
KWA

OSAE-KOMI-WAZA: HOLDING TECHNIQUES

Hon-kesa-gatame
Scarf hold
KEG

Kuzure-kesa-gatame
Modified scarf hold
KKE

Kata-gatame
Shoulder hold
KAG

Kami-shiho-gatame
Top four-corner hold
KSH

Kuzure-kami-shiho-gatame
Modified top four-corner hold
KKS

Yoko-shiho-gatame
Side four-corner hold
YSG

Tate-shiho-gatame
Straight four-corner hold
TSG

Ushiro-kesa-gatame
Reverse scarf hold
UKG

Makura-kesa-gatame
Pillow scarf hold

SHIME-WAZA: STRANGULATION TECHNIQUES (CHOKE LOCKS)

Nami-juji-jime
Normal cross lock
NJJ

Gyaku-juji-jime
Reverse cross lock
GJJ

Kata-juji-jime
Half cross lock
KJJ

Hadaka-jime
Naked lock
HAD

Okuri-eri-jime
Sliding collar lock
OEJ

Kata-ha-jime
Single-wing lock
KHJ

Ryo-te-jime
Two-hands choke
RYJ

Do-jime
Body scissors
DOJ

Tsukkomi-jime
Thrusting choke
TKJ

Kata-te-jime
One-hand choke
KTJ

Sode-guruma-jime
Sleeve wheel choke
SGJ

Sankaku-jime
Triangular choke
SAJ

KANSETSU-WAZA: JOINT TECHNIQUES

Ude-garami
Entangled armlock
UGR

Ude-hishigi-juji-gatame
Cross armlock
JGT

Ude-hishigi-ude-gatame
Arm armlock
UGA

Ude-hishigi-hiza-gatame
Knee armlock
HIG

Ude-hishigi-waki-gatame
Armpit armlock
WAK

Ude-hishigi-hara-gatame
Stomach armlock
HGA

Ude-hishigi-ashi-gatame
Leg armlock
AGA

Ude-hishigi-te-gatame
Hand armlock
TGT

Ude-hishigi-sankaku-gatame
Triangular armlock
SGT

Ashi-garami
Entangled leg lock
AGR

Gokyo No Waza	
5 Groups of instruction—8 techniques in each group	
1.	Deashi-barai, hiza-guruma, sasae-tsurikomi-ashi, uki-goshi, osoto-gari, o-goshi, ouchi-gari, seoi-nage
2.	Kosoto-gari, kouchi-gari, koshi-guruma, tsurikomi-goshi, okuri-ashi-harai, tai-otoshi, harai-goshi, uchi-mata
3.	Kosoto-gake, tsuri-goshi, yoko-otoshi, ashi-guruma, hane-goshi, harai-tsurikomi-ashi, tomoe-nage, kata-guruma
4.	Sumi-gaeshi, tani-otoshi, hane-makikomi, sukui-nage, utsuri-goshi, o-guruma, soto-makikomi, uki-otoshi
5.	Osoto-guruma, uki-waza, yoko-wakare, yoko-guruma, ushiro-goshi, ura-nage, sumi-otoshi, yoko-gake

Atemi Waza – Striking Techniques	
Ude-ate (elbow)	
Yubisaki-ate (fingertip)	Ago-oshi, ryogan-tsuki, suri-age
Kobushi-ate (fist)	Tsuki-kake, tsukiage (kachi-kake), yoko-uchi
Tegatana-ate (outside edge of hand)	Naname-uchi, kirioroshi, ushiro-dori
Hiji-ate (elbow)	Ushiro-ate, ushiro-dori
Ashi-ate (Leg)	
Hiza-gashira-ate (knee)	Ryote-dori, gyakute-dori
Sekito-ate (ball of foot)	Keage, mae-geri, ryote-dori
Kakato-ate (heel)	Ushiro-geri, yoko-geri, ashi-fumi

INDEX

Note: An italicized *f* or *t* following page numbers indicates a figure or table on those pages, respectively.

A

absolute strength 147
achievement goals 143
action–reaction combinations 109–110
Adams, Neil 37
aerobic
   capacity 154
   conditioning 136
   intensity 141
aerobic training 137
agility 136
All-Japan Judo Championships 6
allowing an attack 126
anaerobic conditioning 136
arm armlock 206
armlocks 79
armpit armlock 206
arrogance 29
ashi-garami 206
ashi-guruma 199
ashi-waza 51*t*, 199–200
Asian Games (1958) 6
atemi waza 207
athletes, endurance 137
atrophy 152
attack areas 159
attack technique options 159
attitude, competitive 26–27
attributes, physical 160
attrition, strategy of 162–163
ouchi-gari → kata-guruma 114–115

B

back hip throw 198
back-of-gi grip 95
back throw 201
bag of rice throw 201
balance 75, 136
balanced attack and defense 161
ballistic combinations 111–112
behind-the-neck grip 95
belt drop 196
belt-grab throw 201
belt grip 97
belt lift 186
belt ranking 16
bend to tighten at elbow 103
Berghmans, Ingrid 7
blocks 102
blue judogi 15
body drop 196
body scissors 205
boundary lines 21
bowing
   disregard of in tournaments 9
   etiquette 13
   in competition 15

breakfalls
   backward 72
   forward-falling (mae ukemi) 70
   front-rolling 69
   overview 68
   sideways 71
bridging, turning and 87
Brousse, Michel 9
Budo code of sportsmanship 13

C

carbohydrates 152
catch hands 100
children in judo 30–31, 138, 148
choke locks 205
circular throw 201
Coles, Dave 147
combination attacks 113
combination techniques
   action–reaction 109–110
   ballistic 111–112
   overview 108–109
   transition from one attack to another 112
coming from behind, strategies for 164–165
competition, training for 142–146, 145*t*–146*t*
competitive judo. *See also* etiquette; judo
   attitude 26–27
   contest area specifications 17–18
   making weight 146–147
   penalties 20–21
   rules of 17–18
   scoring 18–20, 21
   stress 27–29
   tips to consider during 168
   training demands of 143
   uncertainty 167–168
   weight classes 6–7
composure 29–30
confidence 28–29, 73
contest area specifications 17–18
controlled practice. *See* yakusoku-renshu
control, positional 79–80
corner drop 196
corner throw 201
counterattacks. *See* counters
counter: cartwheel escape 131
counter: kuchiki-taoshi 130
counters
   allowing an attack 126
   elements necessary for 127
   three lines of defense 125–127, 126*t*
cross armlock 206
cross grip 96
crunching arms 100

D

daki-age 198
daki-wakare 203

Dan grades 16
deashi-barai 199
deashi-barai → sode-tsurikomi-goshi 124
defense, three lines of 126t
deflect hands 101
dehydration 154
dehydration weight loss 149–151
do-jime 205
dojo etiquette 13
dojos
    common rules of 12–13
    definition of 12
    Kodokan 2
double-sleeve grip 97
drills. *See* uchikomi drills

E
ebi (shrimp) movements 88
ECLIPSE program 31
electrolyte balance 154
end-of-sleeve grip 97
endurance athletes 137
energy drinks 155
entangled armlock 206
entangled leg lock 206
environmental limitations 143
etiquette
    dojo 13–14
    in competitive judo 14–17
    overview 12–14
exaggerated right stance 99
exercises, individual. *See* tandoku-renshu (individual
        exercises)

F
favorite technique (tokui-waza) 161
first line of defense 126t
flat position 83
flexibility 136
floating drop 196
floating hip throw 198
floating throw 202
food elements, essential 152. *See also* nutritional
        considerations, during a tournament
food supplements 155–156
foot and leg techniques 51t, 199–200
footwork 74–75
forward foot sweep 199
Franco, Andres 158
freeing leg from side to kesa-gatame 184
freeing leg from side to ushiro-kesa-gatame 185
free practice. *See* randori
Fukuda, Keiko 33
full point (ippon) score 18–20. *See also* scoring ippon

G
Geesink, Anton 6, 7, 15
goals, achievement 143
goal setting 25–26
gokyo no waza 195, 207
Golden Score contest 21
goshin-jutsu 50
Gosselin, Nathalie 31
grading in black-belt Dan ranks 195
grappling techniques
    kansetsu-waza 54t
    osae-komi-waza 53t
    shime-waza 53t–54t
grasping 105–106
grip breaks 101
grip fighting, overemphasizing 106
gripping sequence 90f

grips
    basic 92
    lapel grips 93–94
    pulling-action-of-the-sleeve (hikite) 92
grip strengthening exercises 91
Grossain, Lionel 30
ground fighting
    ebi (shrimp) movements 88
    flat position 83
    guard position 84–85
    half-guard position 86
    holding positions 86
    turning and bridging 87
    turtle position 81–83
ground judo 81
guard position 84–85
gyaku-juji-jime 205

H
hadaka-jime 205
half cross lock 205
half-guard position 86
hand armlock 206
hand techniques 51t, 196–197
hane-goshi 198
hane-goshi-gaeshi 200
hane-makikomi 202
hansoku make. *See* penalties
harai-goshi 198
harai-goshi-gaeshi 200
harai-makikomi 203
harai-tsurikomi-ashi 199
heat exhaustion 150
heel trip 197
high lift 198
high-sleeve grip 96
hikkomi-gaeshi 201
hip spring 198
hip spring counter 200
hip sweep 198
hip sweep counter 200
hip sweep wraparound throw 203
hip transfer 198
hip wheel 198
hiza-guruma 180, 199
holding positions 86
holding techniques 204
hold your lapel 102
hon-kesa-gatame 204
hop around in front → ura-nage 128
hydration 152
hypertrophy 140, 152

I
idori (kneeling posture) 60t
IJF (International Judo Federation) 2, 6
inner-thigh reaping throw 199
inner-thigh reaping throw counter 200
inner-thigh reaping throw slip 197
inner-thigh wraparound throw 202
inner wraparound throw 203
Inokuma, Isao 48
Inoue, Kosei 14
Inouye, Daniel 6
International Judo Federation (IJF) 2, 6
internment camps, Japanese 3, 6
ippon (full point score) 18–20. *See also* scoring ippon
ippon judo 18–20, 158
ippon-seoi-nage 197
ippon-seoi-nage → kouchi-makikomi 117
itsutsu no kata 59, 62t

J

Japanese internment camps 3, 6
jigoku-jime 192–193
jita kyoei 9, 29
joint exercises. *See* sotai-renshu
joint techniques 206
Jordan, Michael 166
judo. *See also* competitive judo
    advancing in 195
    advantages for children 30–31
    as a sport 8–10
    as exercise 32
    basic strategy 172
    broadening your knowledge of 167
    evolution of as a sport 8f
    for police officers 170–181
    for self-defense 170–172
    history of 2
    internationalization of 7–8
    key events in 4f–5f
    limitations of 171
    terminology 16
    women's inclusion in 7, 32–33
    WWII affect on 3, 6
"judo economics" 31–32
judogi, blue 15
judo matches. *See also* Olympic Games
    common terminology of 22
    "Red and White" 17
juji-gatame roll from top 189
ju no kata 59, 64t–65t

K

Kaminaga, Akio 158
kami-shiho-gatame 204
kani-basami 203
Kano, Jigoro 2, 3, 29, 193, 195
kansetsu-waza 206
kata-guruma 196
kata-guruma → crank counter 129
kata-gatame 204
kata-ha-jime 205
kata-juji-jime 205
katame no kata 50
    kansetsu-waza (joint techniques) 54t
    osae-komi-waza (hold-down) 53t
    shime-waza (neck hold lock) 53t–54t
kata-te-jime 205
kata training 48–50, 51t–56t
kawazu-gake 203
Kendrick, James 31–32
Kerr, George 9
kibisu-gaeshi 197
kime no kata 59
    idori (kneeling posture) 60t
    tachiai (standing posture) 61t
Kimura, Masahiko 48
knee armlock 206
knee wheel 199
Kodokan formal exercises. *See* seiryoku zen'yo
    kokumin taiiku
Kodokan goshin-jutsu 55t–56t
Kodokan judo 2, 7, 170
Kodokan self-defense forms. *See* Kodokan goshin-jutsu
Kodokan, the 2, 195
koka 19
kouchi-gari → yoko-tomoe-nage 118
koshi-guruma 198
koshiki no kata 59, 63t
koshi-waza 51t, 198
kosoto-gake 199
kosoto-gake (right) → okuri-ashi-barai (left) 123

kosoto-gari 199
kouchi-gaeshi 200
kouchi-gari 199
kouchi-gari → kata-guruma 122
kouchi-gari → kuchiki-taoshi 119
kouchi-gari → uchi-mata 121
kuchiki-taoshi 197
kuzure-kami-shiho-gatame 204
kuzure-kesa-gatame 204
kuzushi 76, 112
Kyu grades 16

L

lapel grip (tsurite) 93
large hip throw 198
large inner reap 199
large inner reaping throw counter 200
large outer drop 200
large outer reap 199
large outer reaping throw counter 200
large outer wheel 200
large outside wraparound throw 202
large wheel 200
left-side grip 98
leg armlock 206
leg hike 187
leg wheel 199
lifting hip throw 198
lift-pull foot sweep 199
lift-pull hip throw 198
loin or hip techniques 198
long-term goals. *See* goal setting
low-sleeve grip 95

M

MacArthur, Douglas 3
maintaining the lead 164–165
making weight 146–147
makura-kesa-gatame 204
ma-sutemi-waza 52t, 201
Matsumoto, David 9
Maurel, Eric 91
Maximum Efficiency National Physical Education Kata.
    See seiryoku zen'yo kokumin taiiku
mixed martial arts (MMA) 170–171
MMA (mixed martial arts) 170–171
modified scarf hold 204
modified top four-corner hold 204
Moritsugu, Frank 6
morote-gari 183, 197
mountain storm throw 196
moving uchikomi 43
mutual welfare and benefit. *See* jita kyoei

N

nage-komi training 44
nage no kata 50, 51t–52t
Nakamura, Hiroshi 116
naked lock 205
nami-juji-jime 205
New Canadian 6
"nickel and dime" throws 130
normal cross lock 205
nutritional considerations, during a tournament
    153–155

O

obi-otoshi 196
obi-tori-gaeshi 201
off-mat training methods 37
o-goshi 198
o-guruma 200
Okano, Isao 30, 49

okuri-ashi-harai 199
okuri-eri-jime 205
Olympic Games 6–8, 136, 158. *See also* competitive judo
one-armed shoulder throw 197
one-hand drop 197
one-hand lock 205
osae-komi-waza 204
osoto-gaeshi 200
osoto-gari 199
osoto-gari → hiza-guruma 116
osoto-gari (left) feint → seoi-nage (right) 114
osoto-guruma 200
osoto-makikomi 202
osoto-otoshi 200
ouchi-gaeshi 200
ouchi-gari 199
outer wraparound throw 203

P
penalties 20–21
physical attributes 160
police tactics 172–181
positional control 79–80
positions of neutrality 81
positive winning 30
posture 46, 73
post-weigh-in meals 153
power (three-person) uchikomi 41
practice, continual 24–25
practice, controlled. *See* yakusoku-renshu
practice intensity levels 45–46
priority selections 160
proteins 152
pulling-down sacrifice throw 201

R
randori
    blended with kata 50, 51*t*–56*t*
    development examples of 37–38
    goal of 46
    practice intensity 45–46
    regulating resistance in (RRR) 47–48
    tradition of 15
rear trunk turnover 203
"Red and White" judo matches 17
regulating resistance in randori (RRR) 47–48
reverse cross lock 205
reverse scarf hold 204
right stance, exaggerated 99
roll over with space 187
RRR (regulating resistance in randori) 47–48
rules. *See* competitive judo
ryo-te-jime 205

S
sacrifice throws 52*t*. *See also* yoko-sutemi-waza
sambo 17
sankaku-jime 205
sankaku-jime: triangular lock 190–191
sasae-tsurikomi-ashi 199
scarf hold 204
scissors throw 203
scooping throw 196
scoring
    and boundary lines 21
    koka 19
    waza-aris 19
    yuko 19
scoring ippon 18–19, 79
scouting methods 161–162
second line of defense 126*t*
"seiryoku zen'yo" 9
seiryoku zen'yo kokumin taiiku 57, 58*t*–59*t*

self-defense 170–172
self-defense forms, Kodokan. *See* Kodokan goshin-jutsu
self-defense tactics
    against clinch to hadaka-jime 179
    against headlock to ura-nage 177
    against neck grab 178
    against right-handed slap (strike) to osoto-gari 174
    against strike to hiza-guruma 180
    against two-handed push to tomoe-nage 176
    push to waki-gatame 175
self-doubt 28
self-evaluation 166–167
seoi-nage 196
seoi-otoshi 196
shadow uchikomi 41
shido. *See* penalties
shime-waza 205
shizentai 73. *See also* posture
shomen 13
short-term goals. *See* goal setting
shoulder drop 196
shoulder hold 204
shoulder throw 196
shoulder wheel 196
side body wrap 202
side drop 202
side four-corner hold 204
side separation 202
side wheel 202
single-arm push-down 103
single leg entanglement 203
single-wing lock 205
sitting positions 13
sleeve-and-lapel grip 91
sleeve grip 92
sleeve-grip break–cut 105
sleeve-grip break with leg 104
sleeve lift-pull hip throw 198
sleeve-wheel strangle 205
sliding collar lock 205
small inner reap 199
small inner reaping throw counter 200
small outer hook 199
small outer reap 199
sode-guruma-jime 205
sode-tsurikomi-goshi 198
Sone, Koji 5
sotai-renshu 59*t*
soto-makikomi 203
Soviet judo 17
specificity principle 37
speed of attack 142
sports drinks 155
sportsmanship
    and arrogance 29
    Budo code of 13
    jita kyoei 9
springing wraparound throw 202
standing posture 61*t*
stand-up gripping 98
static uchikomi 40
step over → kosoto-gake 127
stiff arms 99
stomach armlock 206
straight four-corner hold 204
strategic variables 159–160
strategy and tactics 158–161
strategy of attrition 162–163
strength 136
strength training 138–140, 139*t*
stress, competitive 27–29

striking techniques 207
Stringer, Corey 150–151
sukui-nage 196
sumi-gaeshi 201
sumi-otoshi 196
supporting foot lift-pull throw 199
swallow counter 200
sweeping ankle foot sweep 199

T
tachiai 61t
tai-otoshi 196
Takada, Yuji 27
Takahashi, Allyn 162
Takahashi, June 33, 48, 49
Takahashi, Masao 6, 10, 170
Takahashi, Phil 91, 117
Takahashi, Ray 14, 27, 38, 166
Takahashi, Tina 7, 30
takedowns 182–183
tandoku-renshu (individual exercises) 58t
tani-otoshi 202
tate-shiho-gatame 204
tawara-gaeshi 201
technical-tactical situations 163–166
technical training. *See also* training methods
    progressive steps for 38–39
"10 and 10 rule" 40
terminology 16, 17, 22, 144
te-waza 51t, 196–197
The Art of War (Tzu) 161
The Fighting Spirit of Judo (Yamashita) 27
the Kodokan 2
third line of defense 126t
throwing mechanics
    kake 78
    kuzushi 76
    tsukuri 77
throwing practice. *See* nage-komi training
throwing techniques
    ashi-waza 51t, 99–100
    koshi-waza 51t
    masutemi-waza 52t
    te-waza 51t, 196–197
    yoko-sutemi-waza 52t
thrusting lock 205
tokui-waza (favorite technique) 161
tomoe-nage 201
top four-corner hold 204
tournament nutritional considerations 153–155
training attitude 24
training for competition 142–146, 145t–146t
training intensity 140–141
training methods. *See also* technical training
    excessive examples of 36
    kata 48–50
    overview 36–38
    randori 15
training plan, development of 143–146, 145t–146t
training, uchikomi. *See* uchikomi training
training variables 140–142, 141t
train weaknesses 160
transition, from one attack to another 112
triangular armlock 206
triangular lock 205
tsubame-gaeshi 200
tsugi-ashi technique 75
tsukkomi-jime 205
tsukkomi-jime counter to waki-gatami 188
tsukuri 77

tsuri-goshi 198
tsurikomi-goshi 198
turning and bridging 87
turn to guard 188
turtle position 82–83
two-handed lapel-break push 104
two-hands lock 205
two-hands reap 197
Tzu, Sun 161

U
uchikomi drills 40–43
uchikomi training 39–40
uchi-makikomi 203
uchi-mata 199
uchi-mata fake → tani-otoshi 120
uchi-mata-gaeshi 200
uchi-mata-makikomi 202
uchi-mata-sukashi 197
uchi-mata → te-guruma 132
uchi-mata → yoko-guruma 133
ude-garami 206
ude-hishigi-ashi-gatame 206
ude-hishigi-hara-gatame 206
ude-hishigi-hize-gatame 206
ude-hishigi-juji-gatame 206
ude-hishigi-sankaku-gatame 206
ude-hishigi-te-gatame 206
ude-hishigi-ude-gatame 206
ude-hishigi-wake-gatame 206
uke, definition of 9
uki-goshi 198
uki-otoshi 196
uki-waza 48–49, 202
uncertainty of sport 167–168
under-elbow grip 96
ura-nage 201
U.S. Catastrophic Sports Injury Research Center 150
ushiro-goshi 198
ushiro-kesaga-gatame 204
utsuri-goshi 198

V
valley drop 202
Van de Walle, Robert 125
$\dot{V}O_2$max 137

W
waza-aris 19
weight control, effective 147
weight gains 151–152
weight-loss practices, study on 147
weight reduction methods 147–150, 151
winning, positive 30
women's inclusion in judo 7, 32–33

Y
yakusoku-renshu 45
yama-arashi 196
Yamashita, Yasuhiro 27, 112
yearly training plan 145t–146t
yoko-gake 202
yoko-guruma 202
yoko-otoshi 202
yoko-shiho-gatame 204
yoko-sutemi-waza 52t, 202–203
yoko-wakare 202
yuko 19

Z
zone tactics 163

ABOUT THE AUTHORS

Masao Takahashi, the family patriarch, has been involved in judo for 65 years, during which time he has taught and coached numerous national and international champions through the Takahashi Martial Arts School. Established in Ontario, Canada, in 1969, this family-run training school is recognized as one of North America's most successful dojos, offering courses in judo, karate, jiu-jutsu, aikido, and kendo. Masao is an 8th-Dan black belt and was decorated by the emperor of Japan in 2002 with the Order of the Sacred Treasure, Gold Rays with Rosette in recognition of his exceptional service to elevating the status of Japanese Canadians through his lifelong commitment to the promotion and development of the sport of judo. He was inducted into the Judo Canada Hall of Fame in 1998.

June Takahashi is a 5th-Dan black belt and a judo instructor at the Takahashi Dojo. She was one of the first women in Canada to earn a black belt and is credited with encouraging and supporting her children's competitive pursuits over the years. The Takahashi siblings, Allyn, Phil, Ray, and Tina, are all accomplished student-athletes who have trained and competed internationally and have earned nine university degrees between them.

Allyn Takahashi is considered the technician of the Takahashi family with a theoretical approach to judo as a sport and a martial art. He was a Canadian national youth champion and wrestler during his high school years, winning three Eastern Canadian Championships and the Canadian National Exhibition International Championship.

Phil Takahashi is a three-time Olympian, two-time medalist in world championship competition, and 10-time Canadian champion. He was inducted into the Judo Canada Hall of Fame in 1996 and currently instructs at the family dojo.

Ray Takahashi is currently a lecturer and wrestling coach at the University of Western Ontario. He is a 3rd-Dan black belt and a three-time Olympian who placed 4th in 1984. A member of the Canadian wrestling team for 10 years, Ray holds 16 Canadian national titles in the sport and was inducted into the Canadian Wrestling Hall of Fame in 1991.

Tina Takahashi is a World University champion who has taught judo for the past 25 years. She was the first women's Sport Canada carded athlete, the first coach of the women's judo team at the 1988 Olympics, and the first Canadian woman to achieve the rank of 6th-degree black belt. In 1998, Tina was inducted into the Judo Canada Hall of Fame.